JAMES BENTLEY

PHOTOGRAPHS BY
HUGH PALMER

THE MOST BEAUTIFUL VILLAGES OF ENGLAND

WITH 285 ILLUSTRATIONS IN COLOUR

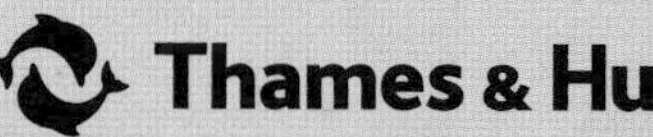

Thames & Hudson

On the cover
(front) *Wherwell, Hampshire*
(back) *Mevagissey, Cornwall*

Half-title page
The English country cottage garden, the inspiration of a whole school of horticulture design; these roses embellish a garden in Lavenham, Suffolk, one of the prettiest villages of East Anglia.

Title pages
The village of Amberley in Sussex nestles among the wooded South Downs. Its church of St. Michael was founded in 681, though most of the present building dates from the Norman Conquest; its castle, visible beyond the trees, is fourteenth-century.

First published in the United Kingdom in 1999 by Thames & Hudson Ltd., 181A High Holborn, London WC1V 7QX

This paperback edition 2009
Reprinted 2011

British Library Cataloguing-in-Publication Data
A catalogue record for this book is available from the British Library
ISBN 978-0-500-28838-2

Printed and bound in Singapore by C.S. Graphics

Author's Acknowledgments

I would like to dedicate the text of this book to John Edward Hawke. I am extremely grateful to Sandie Dawe and her colleague Anne Jenkins at the English Tourist Board for their help in its preparation. My thanks are also due to the East of England Tourist Board (particularly Elaine Simpson), the Northumbria Tourist Board (particularly Valerie Lowther), the North West Tourist Board (particularly Andrea Bingham), the Heart of England Tourist Board (particularly Cathy Harrison), the South East England Tourist Board (particularly Priscilla Chapman), the Southern Tourist Board (particularly Juliette Scott), the Cumbria Tourist Board, the West Country Tourist Board (particularly Robin Deitch-Dey) and the Yorkshire Tourist Board (particularly Susan Kay).

Photographer's Acknowledgments

Discovering the villages of England has been a challenging as well as an enjoyable experience. I quickly found out how little I knew of my own country, and I am very grateful to the fellow photographers who shared their greater knowledge with me: Andrew Lawson, Homer Sykes and Gareth Lovett-Jones. The staff of the English Tourist Board and their regional offices were also extremely helpful in pointing me in the right direction; my thanks to all of them, as well as to the many villagers who put up with my intrusions with such good humour. I was accompanied on many of my trips by my son Ged. A true village boy, he was born shortly after we moved to the country, and watching him grow up in a small rural community has been the greatest pleasure of our time here. These pictures are dedicated to him.

Contents

INTRODUCTION 6

The Northern Counties

Introduction 12

Bamburgh NORTHUMBERLAND 16 · *Chipping* LANCASHIRE 20

Gainford DURHAM 24 · *Hawkshead* CUMBRIA 28

Heptonstall WEST YORKSHIRE 34

Linton-in-Craven NORTH YORKSHIRE 38

Prestbury CHESHIRE 40

The Midland Counties

Introduction 42

Abbots Bromley STAFFORDSHIRE 46 · *Acton Burnell* SHROPSHIRE 50

Chaddesley Corbett WORCESTERSHIRE 54

Cottesbrooke NORTHAMPTONSHIRE 58 · *Dorchester* OXFORDSHIRE 64

Edensor DERBYSHIRE 72 · *Hallaton* LEICESTERSHIRE 74

Southwell NOTTINGHAMSHIRE 78

Welford-on-Avon WARWICKSHIRE 82 · *Weobley* HEREFORDSHIRE 86

The Eastern Counties

Introduction 92

Castle Bytham LINCOLNSHIRE 96 · *Dedham* ESSEX 100

Hemingford Grey CAMBRIDGESHIRE 104

Heydon NORFOLK 108 · *Lavenham* SUFFOLK 114

The Southern Counties

Introduction 122

Aldbury HERTFORDSHIRE 126 · *Amberley* SUSSEX 134 · *Elham* KENT 140

Elstow BEDFORDSHIRE 146 · *Eton* BERKSHIRE 150

Nether Winchendon BUCKINGHAMSHIRE 152 · *Ockley* SURREY 156

Wherwell HAMPSHIRE 158

The Western Counties

Introduction 164

Cerne Abbas DORSET 168 · *Clovelly* DEVON 172

Dunster SOMERSET 180 · *Lacock* WILTSHIRE 186

Lower and Upper Slaughter GLOUCESTERSHIRE 192

Mevagissey CORNWALL 198

Select Bibliography 208

Map 208

Introduction

VILLAGE ENGLAND as we know it is a creation that properly began in Anglo-Saxon times, although you can discover Iron Age and Roman remains in many a small community. Beside the Devonshire village of Clovelly, for instance, Clovelly Dykes is an impressive Iron Age hill fort. And since the name of the Hertfordshire village of Aldbury derives from the Anglo-Saxon for 'old fort', its origins must predate the Anglo-Saxon era.

Anglo-Saxon villagers cultivated their crops by strip farming. In later years open fields provided the villagers with their sustenance, and also helped to transform the shape of ancient places. Other trades were important in those years. Anglo-Saxon Hallaton, for example, prospered on iron-working; today, Hallaton is Leicestershire's loveliest village, and in the parish church you can see Saxon coffin lids. Religion evidently played its part in the foundation of many an English village: Wherwell in Hampshire grew around a nunnery founded in 986; Mevagissey in Cornwall derives its name from two Cornish saints, Mews and Ida.

The villages of England are endowed with countless ecclesiastical treasures. At Aldbury, Hertfordshire, the fine medieval tomb of Sir Robert Whittingham and his wife lies in the church of St. John the Baptist (above). *Linton-in-Craven, Wharfedale, North Yorkshire, has a superb Norman and Early English church – St. Michael and All Angels* (opposite).

Many a Saxon church still stands. The descendants of these first worshippers, as they grew more wealthy, improved what they inherited. The Norman church of St. Michael and All Angels at Linton-in-Craven, North Yorkshire, was begun in the twelfth century, but in the fifteenth the villagers added fine chapels in the Perpendicular style. In spite of the Black Death, which reached England in 1348, and subsequent disastrous policies, such as the enclosures of the eighteenth and nineteenth centuries and the flight to the industrial towns, England's peasantry and yeomanry by no means disappeared. In truth, in some parts of the country sheep farming brought wealth to the countryside, and the architecture of the villages there enormously benefited, especially with the building of magnificent 'wool churches', the finest probably that at Lavenham in Suffolk.

Inside the village churches is preserved a plethora of historic monuments. A particularly delightful one, at Aldbury, in Hertfordshire, is the late fifteenth-century tomb of Sir Robert Whittingham and his wife. Sir Robert's feet rest on a 'green man', the pagan symbol of fertility, who carries a priapic club. In many such churches the lord of the manor or squire sat apart from the rest in a more sumptuous pew. That at Cottesbrooke in Northamptonshire even has a fireplace.

Lower Slaughter in Gloucestershire (above) *stands on the river Eye; its early nineteenth-century corn-mill, although it no longer grinds corn, still retains its water-wheel. The houses of this Cotswold village are built of the warm, honey-coloured stone characteristic of the region.*

With the rise of Methodism, chapels were built to rival the parish church; one of the most interesting is the octagonal chapel of Heptonstall, West Yorkshire. Another example, built in 1839, graces the end of the High Street of Elham in Kent. Other reminiscences of past times in these English villages include tithe barns, such as that at Cerne Abbas in Dorset. They complement remains like the former Benedictine abbey, built in the tenth century at Cerne Abbas, the twelfth-century ruined Torre Abbey at Cockington in Devon, and splendid Lacock Abbey in Wiltshire, which was founded by the Countess of Salisbury in 1232.

Where cattle grazed, leather workers prospered in the villages. Where weavers flourished some of their cottages remain, as in Heptonstall and at Lavenham in Suffolk. Lead mining brought prosperity to Linton-in-Craven, and some of the miners' houses still stand there. For many an English village wheat crops remained important, witness the nineteenth-century corn-mill in Lower Slaughter, Gloucestershire. Often the villager and farmer acquired enough wealth to endow not only their superb churches but also magnificent secular buildings.

Historians have identified four major types of English village. The first group centres on a green or square (created often to accommodate the local market). The second comprises villages which basically stretch along a single street (albeit with a few alleyways sometimes escaping to one or other side). A third group consists of villages which seem to have no plan at all. Finally, there are villages deliberately planned, sometimes by architects whose names we know. Many of these last date from the eighteenth and nineteenth centuries, designed sometimes to house the workers of a great estate.

All of these villages needed at least one inn. And if there was a lord of the manor, then the village still often retains the manor house. That at Lower Slaughter tellingly reveals the social status of the lord and the lesser mortals of the village with an inscription of 1771 in a basement room: 'A good character is valuable to everyone, but especially to servants, for it is their bread and without it they cannot be admitted to a creditable family.'

One more characteristic feature of the English village is the school. These churches and schools sometimes produced geniuses, such as John Bunyan, who was born at Elstow in Bedfordshire. Many village schools were founded out of the munificence of local worthies, such as Edwin Sandys, Archbishop of York, who in 1585 endowed the local school in his birthplace, Hawkshead. So were charitable almshouses, such as that at Linton-in-Craven, founded by Richard Fountaine for six poor women, and the almshouses of 1684 built by John Brabin in Chipping, Lancashire.

Bunyan is a reminder that many an English village has literary associations. Sylvia Plath lies buried in Heptonstall. In the mid eighteenth century Thomas Gray memorably captured a distant prospect of Eton College. William Wordsworth went to school in Hawkshead, now in Cumbria, where you discover the cottage in which he stayed and the desk on which he carved his name. Byron and his mother lived at Southwell in Nottinghamshire. The Victorian novelist Mrs Humphry Ward lived at Aldbury in Hertfordshire. Artists, too, delighted in these communities. John Constable was educated in

At Chipping, in Lancashire, this inscription on the gable-end of a group of stone almshouses commemorates the founder, John Brabin, and the date of his foundation, 1684 (top). *At the church of St. Cassian in Chaddesley Corbett, Worcestershire, the Norman arcade is echoed by an elaborately sculpted font of the same period* (above).

In spite of the blessing of the church, symbolized by the local clergyman leading the revellers during the annual bottle-kicking festival at the ancient village of Hallaton, Leicestershire, the lord of misrule is rarely absent from the traditional festivals of the English village (top *and* above).
The main street of the Exmoor village of Dunster (opposite) *is dominated by its castle and the tower, built in 1775, on Conygar Hill.*

Dedham, Essex, and later his paintings made its church a national landmark. In the same village lived the twentieth-century sporting painter Sir Alfred Munnings.

Although the little-changed, ancient patterns of many of the villages described in this book are endlessly fascinating, it is also worthwhile to seek out later additions. At Lacock in Wiltshire the Old Post Office consists of a couple of eighteenth-century Georgian houses. Prestbury in Cheshire boasts lovely houses of the same period near its river. Dunster in Somerset is enlivened by an eighteenth-century folly. At Hawkshead, in Cumbria, behind an early-Victorian shop front is an eighteenth-century home.

Market day has remained important in many places for bringing villagers together. Many such markets have distant origins. That at Elham in Kent, for example, dates from a charter of 1251. Dunster has an octagonal Yarn Market built at the end of the sixteenth century. The name 'Chipping' (Lancashire) actually means 'market' in old English. Other ancient rites bringing villagers together are the local festivals – perhaps the quaintest is the hare-pie and bottle-kicking festival at Hallaton in Leicestershire.

'England may not unfitly be compared to a house, not very great, but very convenient,' wrote Thomas Fuller in 1662, 'and the several shires may properly be resembled to the rooms thereof.' This book explores the villages of England by way of these shires or counties. In five sections – the Northern Counties, the Midland Counties, the Eastern Counties, the Southern Counties and the Western Counties – it describes and illustrates the most beautiful villages in England, listing them in alphabetical order; there is no question of an order of merit – they are all exquisite. There are, without doubt, many other villages in England which could be described as 'beautiful' and which have not found a place in the present book. However, one of the main principles of selection has been the wish to represent the whole country and to illustrate the very different types of village which are characteristic of contrasting regions.

CASTLE
COFFEE
HOUSE

The Northern Counties

Not surprisingly, the building materials of the villages of the northern counties vary greatly, for they depend on local geology. Lancashire is a land of limestone and sandstone. Millstone grit as well as limestone characterizes Yorkshire, Northumberland and Durham. Sometimes red sandstone appears.

Some villages are especially complex. Even though it is a Cheshire village dating back to Saxon times, Georgian red-brick houses dignify Prestbury, which is located in country famed for its black-and-white timbered houses. The village of Gainford in County Durham has both Georgian and Regency houses. By contrast, the houses of Chipping are built of stone, as are those at Linton-in-Craven (greyer in hue than the Lancastrian examples) across the Pennines in Yorkshire. Evidence of the charitable instincts of past northerners are the early eighteenth-century almshouses at Linton-in-Craven, and the grammar school at Heptonstall, founded in 1642 to give free education to fifty children.

As for the landscape and riverscape, Wharfedale, which shelters the village of Linton-in-Craven, is one of England's most entrancing river valleys. Much of the countryside of Lancashire is moorland, with stone-built villages. Move into Cumbria and discover the waters of the Lake District and in particular the village of Hawkshead. Small wonder that William Wordsworth, who was educated and lived here, pined from abroad for his England. Oddly enough, the narrow ginnels (alleyways) leading to courtyards in peaceful Hawkshead were designed to defend the village from Scots marauders. Another witness to the need to defend these villages from enemies is the glowering presence of Bamburgh Castle in Northumberland. These northern counties have always cherished their independence, as Henry Adams wrote of Yorkshire in 1906, 'To a certain degree, evident enough to Yorkshiremen, Yorkshire was not English – or was all England, as they might choose to express it.'

The Elizabethan church of St. Michael and All Angels (opposite) *at Hawkshead, in Cumbria, was founded in 1150 and is especially famous for its literary associations. Its graveyard is overlooked by such Lake District daffodils as William Wordsworth so memorably eulogized, and on the east wall are set stone seats where he would sit and meditate. In Wordsworth's time such churches were usually whitewashed; indeed, the poet once described this one as 'the snow white church upon her hill.' The north aisle was rebuilt in 1578 at the expense of Archbishop Edwin Sandys of York, who founded here the school which Wordsworth attended.*

The quintessential northern village – stone buildings set among wooded hills; at Burnsall (left) *an impressive five-arched bridge spans the river Wharfe. The theme of stone is repeated in the houses and the local post office of Bainbridge, while the snowmen at Linton-on-Craven are a reminder that winters in the north of England can be severe, although clearly enjoyable.*

The monument to Grace Darling in Bamburgh churchyard (below) *preserves her memory; her grave can also be found in the churchyard of the thirteenth-century St. Aidan (named after the missionary who died here in 651)* (right).

Bamburgh
NORTHUMBERLAND

BAMBURGH CASTLE was the home of the earliest kings of Northumbria. Massive, built of stone, the castle sits 150 feet above the turbulent sea, stretching for a quarter of a mile along its cliff. Its origins date back to 547, when an Anglo-Saxon leader, Ida, built here a wooden fort. Sir Lancelot is said to have eloped to this castle with King Arthur's wife, Guinevere.

Its fortunes proved fickle: ruined by the Vikings in 993; rebuilt by Henry II; demolished by Edward IV during the Wars of the Roses. Bought in 1893 by the first Lord Armstrong, it was lavishly restored, its King's Hall boasting carved teak, its armoury intact, its well some 150 feet in depth. The superb Norman keep and much of the curtain-wall survived this restoration.

The village rejoices in the memory of Grace Darling, born here in 1815. On 7 September 1838, at the age of twenty-three, she rowed out with her father, who was keeper of the Longstone lighthouse of the Farne Islands, to rescue five people from the wrecked steamer *Forfarshire.* The boat in which they achieved this feat is now in Bamburgh Museum, opposite the church of St. Aidan. Close by, a plaque indicates Grace Darling's birthplace. She died a mere three years after the rescue. Her grave and monument are in St. Aidan's churchyard, a church with a thirteenth-century crypt and chancel.

Grey-stone cottages grace Bamburgh, some alongside inns surrounding the wooded green, which is known as The Grove.

Craggy Bamburgh Castle protects the sturdy though often elegant homes of the village (right). *Its ramparts* (above), *in part rebuilt in the nineteenth century but retaining their early thirteenth-century curtain-wall, still glower over the coastline.*

The powerful presence of the foursquare keep (above) *finds an echo in the strong stone walls of local houses* (left *and* above left).

Chipping LANCASHIRE

CHESTNUT TREES and a fast-flowing brook lend immediate charm to this village. 'Chipping' in old English means 'market', and in all probability around a market this village developed. Then, in the seventeenth century Chipping began to prosper from the wool trade, maintained by the fleeces of the sheep which grazed on the Bowland Fells. In consequence, many of the village's finest buildings also date from the seventeenth century.

Undoubtedly, Chipping's most generous benefactor was the seventeenth-century dyer and cloth merchant, John Brabin. As an inscription reveals, he lived at 22 Talbot Street. When Brabin died in 1683, his will (which he had written the previous year, 'being infirm of body') bequeathed money to ease the plight of the poor and also to build a village school. You can discern John Brabin's name, as well as the date 1684, on the gable end of a group of stone-built, terraced almshouses, which were also built with his money.

Cobbled Windy Street is charming; some of the stone-built houses, with their mullioned windows, are set at right-angles to the street amid little gardens. Windy Street reaches Talbot Street, which then stretches down to a bridge over Chipping Brook, from which you can see an ancient water-mill with a water-wheel and, further in the distance, Longridge Fell.

Although the church, dedicated to St. Bartholomew, was founded in 597, its present tower dates from the mid fifteenth century and the rest (restored in 1873) from 1506. It is home to some of the local traditional spindle-backed chairs, while stained-glass windows commemorate recent celebrated practitioners of this art. Buried in the chancel is The Rev. John King, who was vicar here from 1622 to 1672 and survived all the religious vicissitudes of that turbulent era.

Beneath the Lancashire fells sits the village of Chipping in the valley of the Hodder. In the centre of this rugged yet idyllic scene rises the tower of the church of St. Bartholomew.

LONGRIDGE
WINDY STREET

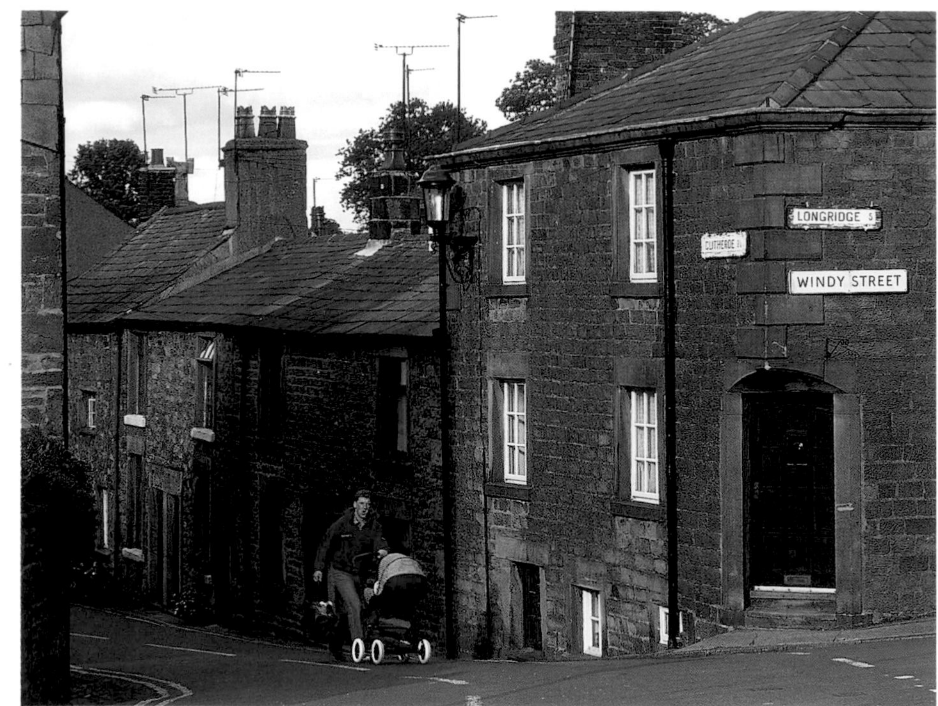

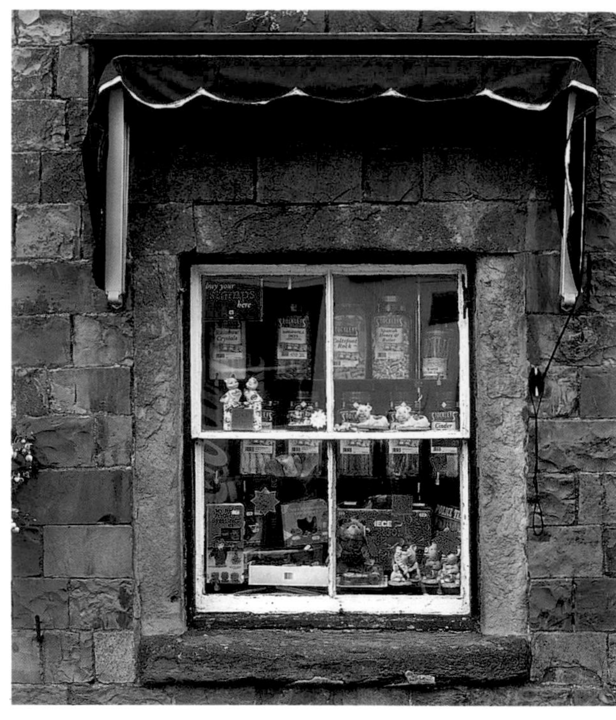

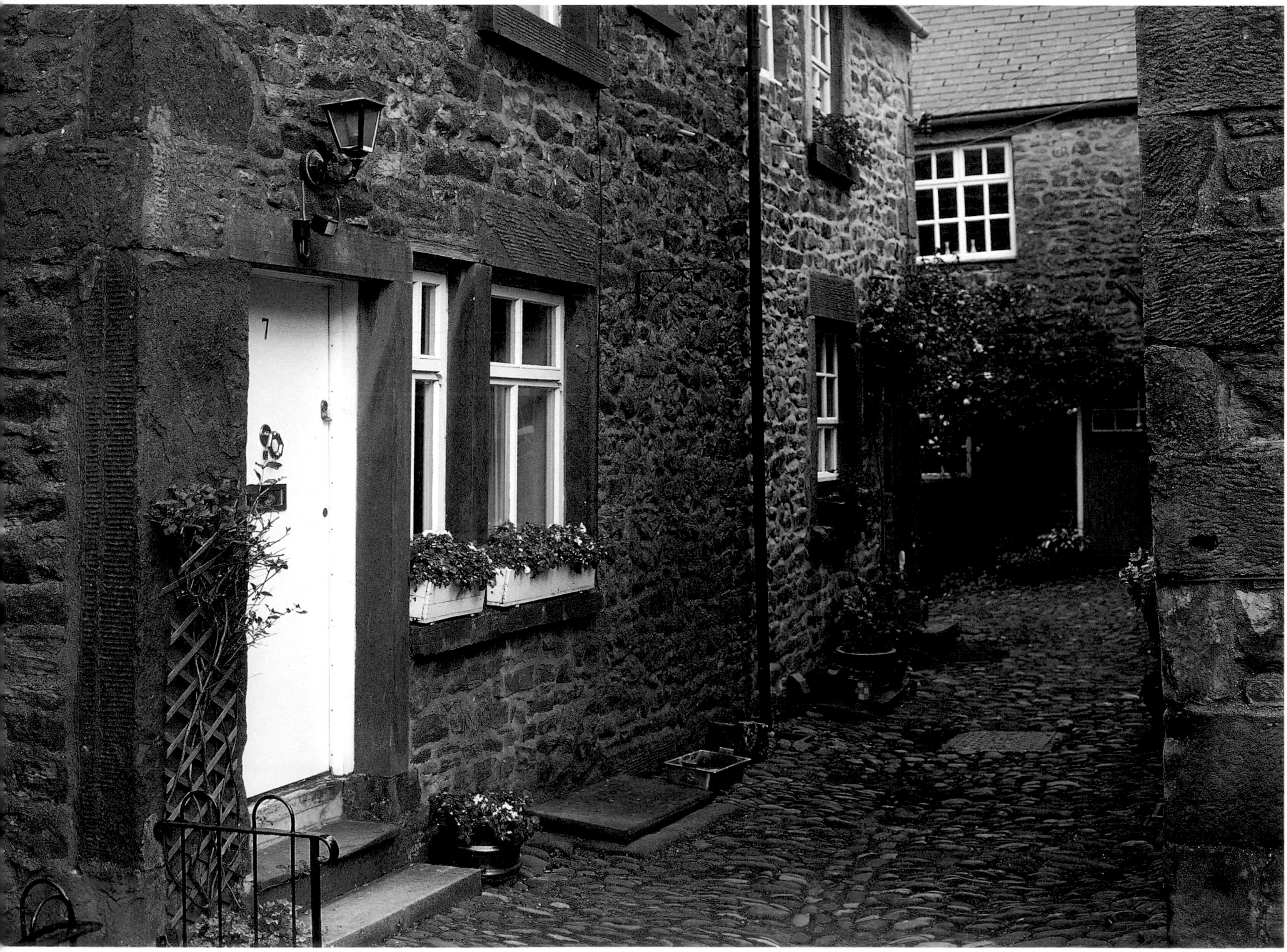
7

The mostly stone-built houses of Chipping (these pages) *are endowed with a sturdy appeal. Well-maintained façades make this village a special delight.*

Gainford DURHAM

ALTHOUGH Gainford was founded by the Saxons, its greatest era of prosperity occurred during the eighteenth and early nineteenth centuries, and this is reflected in its architecture, with Georgian and Regency buildings adding their charm to the sloping village green. Two of the village's gems are the so-called Georgian House and the early eighteenth-century St. Colette's school. Further evidence of past prosperity is Gainford Spa, beside the river Tees, which also flourished in the eighteenth and early nineteenth centuries.

But earlier buildings still remain. Gainford Hall was built at the beginning of the seventeenth century, embellished with mullioned and transomed windows, as well as gables, tall chimneys and a dovecote. From here, High Row winds to the timbered *Cross Keys* inn. This is a splendid street: terraced houses with gardens, and courtyards to the rear. Rising above the Tees beside the village green is the thirteenth-century parish church of St. Mary. Inside are a Jacobean font cover and a monument to the Middleton family. Travel two miles west to discover at Winston a Jacobean mansion, Westholme Hall, built in 1606, and a bridge with a single span built across the Tees in 1764.

Set in delightful countryside near the river Tees (opposite), *Gainford's grey-stone houses are grouped around the sloping village green and the parish church of St. Mary* (above *and* left). *Upriver is Gainford Spa, much favoured by those who took the therapeutic waters in the eighteenth and nineteenth centuries.*

Much of the charm of English villages is derived from the variety of their vernacular architecture, and Gainford is no exception.

The timbered Cross Keys *inn* (left) *(the name is derived from the insignia of the Papacy) is but one of the fine buildings reached along Gainford's winding High Street. The green* (above) *still serves its traditional function as a centre of village life.*

*T*he village of Hawkshead (opposite) *lies enfolded in the rugged Cumbrian hills. The interior of the parish church of St. Michael and All Angels* (left) *boasts sturdy pillars and low arches; murals on the whitewashed walls date from the seventeenth and eighteenth centuries. Look out also for Biblical inscriptions and, among the many monuments, the effigies of the parents of Archbishop Edwin Sandys in the chapel at the east end of the north aisle.*

Hawkshead

CUMBRIA

OCCUPYING a dramatic site in the Lake District, Hawkshead looks out to Esthwaite Water, which laps the southern tip of the village; the hills of Grizedale Forest also run southwards. The village is roughly halfway between Windermere and Coniston Water. Walk the mile-long footpath which leads west from the village to Hawkshead Hill for magnificent views of the surrounding mountains.

Here at the age of eight William Wordsworth came for his schooling, having been born at Cockermouth in 1770. For the most part he stayed here before going up to Cambridge seven years later. Somewhere in the warren of narrow, sometimes cobbled streets, with little squares and courtyards reached beneath low arches, is Ann Tyson's cottage, with its flight of outdoor steps, set where Vicarage Lane meets present-day Wordsworth Street, where the poet is said to have made his home. As for the refurbished schoolhouse (now a museum), you enter it by a door underneath a sundial to discover the original desks, on one of which Wordsworth carved his name. Another author, Beatrix Potter, who published her first book *The Tale of Peter Rabbit* in 1902, lived close by Hawkshead, at Hill Top Farm, a seventeenth-century farmhouse a couple of miles from the main part of the village.

Just above the school rises the parish church of St. Michael and All Angels. One of its chapels is dedicated to William and Margaret Sandys, the parents of Edwin Sandys, who was born at Esthwaite Hall in 1516 and became Archbishop of York. Edwin Sandys founded the local school in 1585. Although the first church on this site was consecrated in the mid twelfth century, the present building dates mostly from the sixteenth. The painting of its murals began in 1711.

The Lakeland poet, William Wordsworth, declared that his heart would fill with pleasure and dance with the daffodils; these grow appropriately above the church of St. Michael and All Angels (left). *Here, the poet would have known the village's characterful houses* (above).

Queen's
SOCCER

Hawkshead's warren of twisting streets, which include one named after the village's most illustrious son (left), *offer the visitor sudden, exquisite tableaux, such as this curio shop window* (opposite) *or flower-bedecked façades* (above).

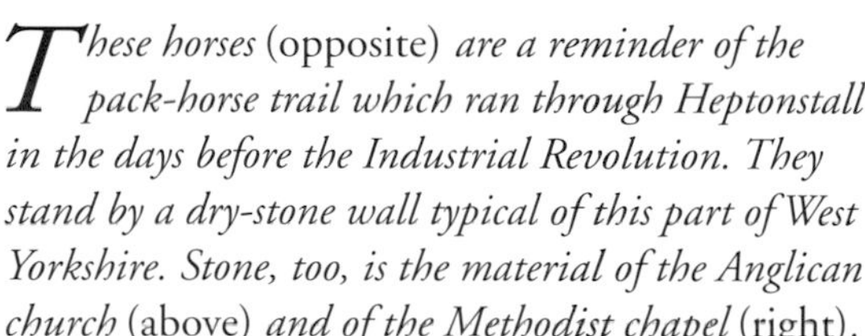

These horses (opposite) *are a reminder of the pack-horse trail which ran through Heptonstall in the days before the Industrial Revolution. They stand by a dry-stone wall typical of this part of West Yorkshire. Stone, too, is the material of the Anglican church* (above) *and of the Methodist chapel* (right).

Heptonstall

WEST YORKSHIRE

THE PACK-HORSE TRAIL, running a steep mile from Heptonstall to connect the village with Hebden Bridge, and the once vital Rochdale Canal indicate the importance of the wool trade, created by hand-loom weavers, on which these West Yorkshire towns and villages depended in past times. During the English Civil War Royalist troops occupied Hebden Bridge and in 1643 were unwise enough to try to storm some of Oliver Cromwell's Roundheads (who had invested Heptonstall) by climbing this pack-horse trail. Inevitably, the Roundheads had the advantage and the Royalists suffered extensive casualties.

The most fascinating building in Heptonstall is its octagonal Wesleyan Methodist chapel, whose foundation stone was laid by John Wesley himself in 1764. A second church, dating from the thirteenth century, is in ruins. Beside it the architects Mallinson and Healy built a Perpendicular Gothic church in the mid nineteenth century. Both the ruin and the new church are dedicated to St. Thomas. But above all it is the old weavers' cottages which add charm to the village.

The former grammar school of Heptonstall is now a museum. Founded by a local clergyman in 1642, it offered free education to fifty children and only closed in 1889. Rebuilt in the early eighteenth century, it is situated in picturesquely named Churchyard Bottom. This is not, however, the only quaint name in this village, for the narrow main street is called Towngate and Top o' th' Town. Seek out the new churchyard to find the grave of the poet Sylvia Plath, who died in 1963 in her thirty-first year. Do not neglect Hebden Bridge, with its terraced cottages sheltered in a valley.

Heptonstall is surrounded by open land, crossed by traditional dry-stone walls, a background to two forms of leisure (above *and* right). *The octagonal Methodist chapel* (opposite) *has a foundation stone laid by John Wesley himself in 1764; note the mighty pulpit, symbol of Wesley's emphasis on preaching the Word of God, and the organ, a reminder of the Wesleyan love of music and of the hymnologist Charles Wesley.*

Linton-in-Craven

NORTH YORKSHIRE

Soft winter snow coats the walls and grey-stone houses of Linton-in-Craven (below). *Resplendent Fountaine's Hospital* (opposite) *was founded through the munificence of Sir Richard Fountaine in 1721.*

GREY-STONE HOUSES, some clad with ivy, group themselves around the village green of Linton-in-Craven, in Upper Wharfedale. Three bridges span the little boulder-strewn stream that runs through the village: a modern one for road traffic, a 'clapper bridge' (so named from the long flat stones with which it was built) and a pack-horse bridge.

Fountaine's Hospital is the finest building in this village, with a most impressive façade and a splendid voluted tower with a dome. It takes its name from Richard Fountaine, who founded it in 1721 as an almshouse for six poor women. Today the Hospital also houses men. Some experts believe it was designed by the English Baroque architect Sir John Vanbrugh, and it certainly is in his style. Whoever the architect, he clearly intended to offer the village a virtual stage setting, for behind the façade he was far less flamboyant. His rusticated archway leads to the chapel, whose east window is Venetian in style.

On the other side of the village green is the late seventeenth-century Linton Hall. Its gable curves magnificently; some of its windows were modified in the Georgian era without disrupting the harmony of the whole; another charming feature is a doorway with a semicircular pediment.

Beside the river Wharfe rises the parish church of St. Michael and All Angels. Its corbelled bell-cote is like a pyramid. The church as it stands today dates mainly from the fourteenth century; the windows of the west aisle are from the very beginning of that century. But go inside to discover that some of its stones take the visitor back as far as the twelfth century. The font is Norman, as are the chancel arch and a couple of bays; and there are fifteenth-century Perpendicular chapels.

National
Westminster
Bank

Prestbury CHESHIRE

THE DELIGHTFUL VILLAGE is built around a green and main street which runs down to a bridge spanning the river Bollin. The houses close by the bridge are mostly Georgian and built of mature red brick, contrasting with the three-storeyed timber-framed house by the church (which once was the home of the parish priest) as well as with the bow-fronted houses in the main street. The present handsome vicarage was built by Ernest Newton in 1893. Note a fine, early-Victorian, three-storeyed gabled house at the south end of this fascinating street.

St. Peter's church has a fine twelfth-century Norman chapel (detached from the main building), in part rebuilt in 1747. Its west doorway remains unchanged, with typical Norman zig-zag and pellet ornamentation as well as, in the tympanum, Christ sculpted in a halo. But Prestbury's origins predate the Norman Conquest, a fact revealed by the remains of a Saxon cross discovered in the churchyard in 1841.

To explore this mainly thirteenth-century church is especially rewarding, since its furnishings and architectural details date from its origins to the present day. Its west tower was built in the late fifteenth century. Inside are early eighteenth-century wall-paintings depicting the Twelve Apostles. The arcades are both thirteenth-century, one with octagonal and round piers, the other with quatrefoil piers. The pulpit dates from 1607, and there are Jacobean pews and brass chandeliers. Sir George Gilbert Scott and John Oldrid Scott restored the church in the late nineteenth century and have left us their own addition: the five-light east window.

Half-timbering and brick make Prestbury's High Street an interesting mix of styles (left)*. The porch of the Norman chapel* (above)*, created around 1190, stands in the churchyard of the parish church.*

The Midland Counties

THE VILLAGES of these English counties delight in peerless building materials. At Weobley in Herefordshire are half-timbered black-and-white houses (the timbers carefully dividing the whitewashed walls into panels a metre or so square). And in Warwickshire Henry James declared, 'I have interviewed the genius of pastoral Britain.' A special delight at Chaddesley Corbett in Worcestershire is the timber-framed fourteenth-century *Talbot Inn*. Visit Hallaton in Leicestershire to see purple bricks, created in the fiercest part of a kiln, which were used in the eighteenth century to create chequer patterns on the houses. Abbots Bromley in Staffordshire started life as a village of timber-framed houses (note the village school of 1606), but at the beginning of the seventeenth century it turned to brick.

As elsewhere in England, such villages in past times needed to protect themselves against predators; the village of Acton Burnell in Shropshire sheltered under the walls of a now ruined thirteenth-century castle. As another reminder of the violence of the past, Chaddesley Corbett in Worcestershire has a parish church dedicated to a schoolmaster-saint murdered in the village; at the time of the Reformation Roman Catholic priests were particularly endangered, witness the priests' holes in nearby Harvington Hall. Some of these Midland villages are dominated by one superb ecclesiastical building, the most astounding at Southwell in Nottinghamshire; a second masterpiece is the church of Dorchester in Oxfordshire, with its fine windows.

And rivers play their part in the charm of these counties. Derbyshire and Staffordshire are divided by the river Dove and its often rugged valley. Shropshire is bisected by the river Severn. Four tributaries, the Cherwell, the Thame, the Evenlode and the Windrush, feed the Thames in Oxfordshire. No fewer than seven rivers flow through Herefordshire. And these rivers have proved vital to the English village. Without the Thame, for instance, it is unlikely that a religious community would have settled in the village of Dorchester and bequeathed us its superb abbey church.

Half-timbered houses, like this fine example (opposite) *at Wilmcote, Warwickshire, characterize the villages of this part of England.*

Scenes from the Midlands: Southwell Minster (left) *is a totally unexpected sight in a Nottinghamshire village; a lych-gate* (top) *guards the way to the Perpendicular Gothic church of the Warwickshire village of Henley-in-Arden; this pretty thatched cottage graces Hallaton in Leicestershire* (above).

Abbots Bromley

STAFFORDSHIRE

A SIX-SIDED timber building was once the medieval trading centre of Abbots Bromley. For many years the village was dominated by the Bagot family, whose Elizabethan home still stands here. They built the market-hall in the fifteenth century. In 1705 the Bagot family also endowed the village almshouses. King Richard II was welcomed here to hunt and in recompense gave the family a herd of goats, whose descendants are still kept in the park of the ancestral home.

In the parish church are six sets of reindeer horns. Once a year, in September, twelve dancers and musicians, wearing Tudor dress, bring them out to perform the Abbots Bromley horn dance: six of them carry the antlers on their shoulders; another performer carries on his shoulders a hobby horse; one performs as a 'fool', colourfully dressed; a boy bears a bow and arrows; a woman dresses as Maid Marion; the dancers then undertake an eight-mile tour of local farms.

The parish church is dedicated to St. Nicholas. Medieval, with an early eighteenth-century tower built to replace one which fell down in 1688, topped with balustrades and urns, it was brilliantly restored in the mid nineteenth century by G. E. Street. The chancel is particularly magical. Do not miss the superb nineteenth-century stained-glass by Burlison and Grylls in the east window. Another fine nineteenth-century building is the chapel designed for the Woodard School for Girls (which was founded in 1874) by R. H. Carpenter and built between 1875 and 1881.

The six-sided former market-hall (left *and* above) *of Abbots Bromley stands at the heart of the village. The eighteenth-century, Queen Anne-style tower of the parish church rises just above the trees* (opposite).

Village cottages and this overhanging, half-timbered house in Bagot Street (above *and* right) *charmingly illustrate the different materials used in the buildings of Abbots Bromley.*

Yet more delightful variations on the architectural themes of the village (left *and* below)*; the Bagots are remembered on the façade of the village almshouses* (below left) *which were endowed by the family in 1705. Reindeer horns are kept in the parish church to await the annual horn dance* (above).

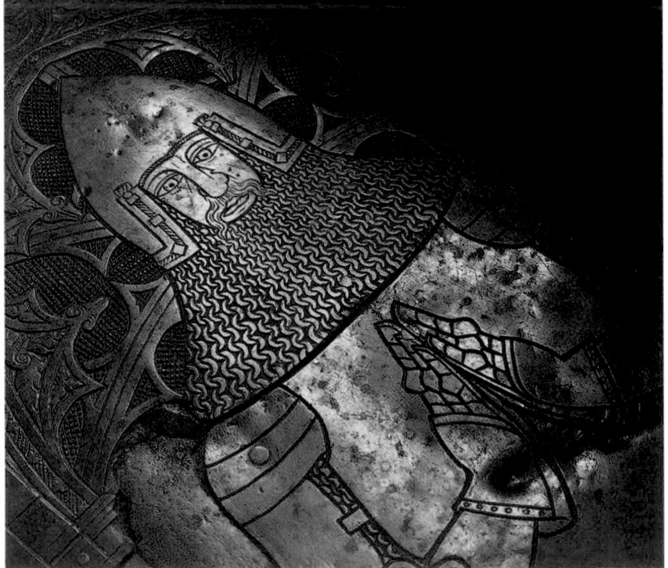

Acton Burnell

SHROPSHIRE

A RUINED RED SANDSTONE CASTLE indicates the former political and social importance of the village of Acton Burnell. It was built in the mid twelve-eighties on behalf of the Bishop of Bath and Wells, Robert Burnell, who was also Lord Chancellor of England in the reign of Edward I. The castle dominates Acton Burnell Hall, an early nineteenth-century construction. This Georgian building is surrounded by a wooded park which incorporates two lakes and a folly. The castle also surveys the grey-green stone and the timber-framed black-and-white cottages of the village.

St. Mary's church, apart from its nineteenth-century tower, dates almost totally from the thirteenth century. Inside are memorials not only to the Burnells but also to the Lee family, who were lords of this village in the seventeenth century. One lovely monument, to Sir Humphrey Lee, is by Nicholas Stone. Their successors include Richard Henry Lee, who signed the American Declaration of Independence in 1776, and General Robert E. Lee, who commanded the army of the South during the American Civil War. Sir Richard Lee's monument dates from 1591. Do not miss the altogether magnificent monumental brass of Sir Nicholas Burnell, who died in 1382.

South of the village stands the early seventeenth-century Langley Chapel, with contemporary furnishings, and the gatehouse and walls of Langley Hall. A mile north of the village, the church of Pitchford has a wooden monument to a knight, carved in the mid thirteenth century, and a half-timbered manor house built in 1473.

Among the treasures of St. Mary's church are a monumental brass (left) *of Sir Nicholas Burnell, and a sixteenth-century monument to Sir Richard Lee* (above). *The castle* (opposite), *the oldest fortified manor house in England, was finished in 1284, a year after Edward I visited the Burnells' previous home on this spot.*

Fine box pews in the nearby seventeenth-century Langley Chapel (opposite) *indicate the relative social importance of those who worshipped in them by their size. Half-timbering of amazing complexity graces nearby Pitchford Hall* (above), *while a more modest variety has been applied to the village houses* (left).

Chaddesley Corbett

WORCESTERSHIRE

The houses of Church Row (below) *form an entrancing sight in the village. Equally attractive are those which abut the church of St. Cassian* (opposite), *distinguished by its graceful eighteenth-century spire. The church also has a Norman font* (see page 9) *and arcade.*

THE HALF-TIMBERED cottages of Chaddesley Corbett co-exist happily with the other ancient buildings of the village, one of the finest being the fourteenth-century, timber-framed *Talbot Inn.* More recent buildings in the pleasant main street are built of brick and date from the Georgian period, while the three brick cottages constituting the Charity House were built in the early nineteenth century. Lych-gate House, opposite, is early Georgian. The misnamed Tudor House dates in fact from the mid eighteenth century.

The parish church, like the *Talbot Inn,* also dates from the fourteenth century, though it was begun by the Normans. Its dedication, to St. Cassian, is unique in the Christian world, for he was murdered in this village – a Christian schoolmaster knifed by his pagan students. The font is earlier than the present church, dating from the twelfth century, four dragons carved on its bowl. An eighteenth-century west tower rises above the church, itself topped by a spire. The chancel is outrageously beautiful, in the Decorated style with an east window of five lights. Here are Norman motifs, arcades, aisles and arches, as well as a Gothic sedilia, piscina and aumbry.

North-west of Chaddesley Corbett stands the multi-gabled, Tudor Harvington Hall, a moated manor house. Its lake feeds the moat. Inside are Elizabethan frescoes, priest holes and secret passages, built when Catholic priests were proscribed in England and often needed to hide from their persecutors. (The house belonged to the Roman Catholic Throckmortons, one of whom, Francis, was executed in 1584 for writing in code to Mary Queen of Scots.) Modified in the eighteenth century, the hall has been well restored. There is a nature reserve to the east at Chaddesley Wood, set up in 1973 to protect the oak forest.

A magical amalgam of styles marks the houses of this street in Chaddesley Corbett (above), *some of Georgian brick, others half-timbered or rendered and colour-washed, while* (opposite) *we see the so-called Tudor House, the general stores shop and the Lych-gate House (looking across to the fourteenth-century* Talbot Inn*).*

D.BANKS

SAMUEL JUKES

Cottesbrooke

NORTHAMPTONSHIRE

COTTESBROOKE HALL was built in the reign of Queen Anne on behalf of Sir John Langham. It has seven bays and two storeys decorated with Corinthian pilasters; its entrance has Corinthian columns. The entrance hall was stuccoed in the middle of the eighteenth century and its fireplace dates from a couple of decades later. Another eighteenth-century fireplace decorates the library, a third the ballroom. The staircase is Rococo. Some hold that this house served as the model for Jane Austen's *Mansfield Park*. In typical eighteenth-century fashion, the gardens to the south of the hall have statues of Socrates, Homer, the Attic orator Lycurgus and the Theban general and statesman Epaminondas.

Of the village parish church of All Saints, John Betjeman noted that it is secluded, in a hollow amongst Irish yews, and is not remarkable save for its extraordinary seventeenth-century Langham pew, in two storeys with its fireplace, and opposite a three-decker pulpit. Betjeman added, 'The other fittings, including the box pews in the nave, have managed to survive the Gothic which attacked less lonely spots in the last century.'

All Saints is cruciform and mostly dates from the thirteenth century, although it was comprehensively restored in the late nineteen-fifties. Among its splendid monuments is one to Sir John Langham, created by Thomas Cartwright Sen. in 1676. Another to John Rede, who died in 1604, includes the figures of ten kneeling children.

Cottesbrooke Hall is a superb example of the Queen Anne style, surrounded by magnificent landscaped gardens.

Battlemented, tree-sheltered, the parish church of All Saints at Cottesbrooke (above) *houses the tomb of John Rede* (left). *This village has exquisite houses, some of them thatched* (far left) *and some of them belonging to the estate* (opposite page).

Traditionally, not only the riders and their horses but the whole village participates in a local hunt, such as this one at Cottesbrooke, about to move off from a lawn meet.

THE POST OFFICE
Dorchester-on-Thames Post Office
Antiques
WAR MEMORIAL
OPEN

Dorchester

OXFORDSHIRE

In Saxon times the gentle village of Dorchester, situated on the west bank of the river Thame, was a city, its cathedral controlling a diocese stretching as far as Yorkshire. After the Norman Conquest the see was transferred to Lincoln. In 1170 the Norman conquerors founded an Augustinian abbey on the site of the cathedral. It was embellished in the next two centuries and today stands as the majestic abbey church of St. Peter and St. Paul.

Its fourteenth-century stained-glass in the three east windows is magical, the finest the Decorated north Jesse window; this traces Jesus's family tree, the members perching on the branches of a tree which rises from the body of his ancestor Jesse. Some of the figures are in stained-glass, others in stone. At the top of the tree is Jesus himself. The lead font dates from around 1180.

You enter and leave the churchyard by an oak lych-gate designed by the eminent Victorian architect William Butterfield in 1852. Note the fourteenth-century gabled building in the churchyard, once Dorchester's village school. The second gabled building in view is *The George Hotel* opposite the lych-gate. Historians speculate that this may have been part of the fifteenth-century abbey. Its overhanging upper storey presages many other delightful buildings in the cobbled High Street, some brick-built and timber-framed, the most notable *The White Hart*, a seventeenth-century coaching-inn.

The lanes which lead off to either side of the High Street are lined with seventeenth-century thatched cottages. Look out for no fewer than seven in Malthouse Lane. In Samian Way Molly Mop's Cottage, with its thatched roof and walls of flint and patterned red brick, was built in 1701.

Ancient Dorchester is represented by a hundred-acre site beside the Thame enclosed by a ditch, known as Dyke Hills, dating from the Iron Age, and by the remains of a third-century Roman wall. The High Street follows the former Roman road.

The quintessentially English village High Street of Dorchester (opposite), *with its half-timbered and gabled houses, shelters under the massive parish church.* The George Hotel (below) *proclaims its status as a former coaching-inn. Note the wide arch, capable of allowing coaches through to the interior courtyard. The abbey church* (overleaf), *by the river Thame, first attracted monks to this place; the church is built of stone ferried down the river.*

Among the monuments of Dorchester's church is this late thirteenth-century effigy (above) *of a stone knight who seems determined to rise from death and begin fighting again. The church also has a Romanesque font in lead* (right). *But its greatest glory is the Decorated east window* (far right), *depicting the Tree of Jesse, its branches imitated in the stonework. The door* (opposite) *is adorned with magnificent metalwork.*

FREDERICK SELLWOOD.
SIDNEY A WILLIAMS.
OWEN WHITING.
WALTER L. WOOD.
1939 – 1945
STANLEY ATKINS
STANLEY BARTON
RONALD BIRCH
VINCENT HAZLEDINE

Since World War I, a stone cross has featured on many an English village green (opposite). *The houses surrounding the cross at Dorchester display entrancingly varied styles, as do these cottages* (left *and* below).

Chatsworth House (opposite), *built in 1707 for the first Duke of Devonshire, overlooks the extraordinary village of Edensor* (this page) *which the sixth Duke commissioned to be built in the early nineteenth century. Among its varied delights are Sir George Gilbert Scott's parish church, soaring above houses built in a variety of styles.*

Edensor
DERBYSHIRE

THIS DERBYSHIRE VILLAGE is architecturally unique. In the early nineteenth century the sixth Duke of Devonshire, annoyed that the village blocked one of his favourite views from the great house of Chatsworth, had the whole group of buildings moved west to another part of his park.

The architect John Robertson of Derby then created new buildings, their styles a *mélange* of what was fashionable at the time: Romanesque; medievally castellated; embellished with Tudor chimneys; decorated with gables in the Jacobean fashion; enlivened with Georgian doorways; some houses Italian in style; others with roofs resembling those of Swiss chalets. The Duke did not stint on cost: the stone was of the very best quality; the details were carved meticulously.

Later, in 1867, Giles Gilbert Scott designed for the village a magnificent Early English Gothic church. Its tower and spire proclaim its importance, as it dominates the village. In its graveyard you can find the tomb of the Duke's superb gardener, Sir Joseph Paxton, designer of Crystal Palace. To Paxton we owe the spaciousness of this village and the laburnum-planted village green. Scott incorporated in the chapel earlier monuments, notably one of 1625 in the Lady Chapel to the first Earl of Devonshire, William Cavendish, and to his brother. Look out for a monumental brass to John Beaton (steward to Mary Queen of Scots) who died in 1570. Another grave is that of Kathleen Kennedy, sister of the former American president, who was killed in a French aircraft accident in 1948. She lies here because of her marriage to the Marquis of Hartington, a brother of the Duke of Devonshire. A plaque recalls the visit of President J. F. Kennedy to her grave.

Climb the lane which connects the main street to see Chatsworth and the Derwent valley – a truly splendid view of the house.

Hallaton's green is remarkable for its conical 'butter cross' (above). *Terraces of dainty cottages line the tranquil churchyard* (right *and* opposite).

Hallaton
LEICESTERSHIRE

HALLATON is mentioned in the Domesday Book (as 'Alctone') but was undoubtedly settled much earlier, for when the railway was built across the Welland valley in 1878, clothing and pottery dating back to the Roman occupation of England were discovered.

The Welland valley forms the background to this village (though it lies in hilly country). Its parish church of St. Michael and All Angels was begun in the twelfth century. The west tower and broach spire (a spire without a parapet) were built in the next century. The aisles date from the fourteenth century, with a little crypt in the north aisle. The church clock peals a chime every three hours, to which the villagers rhyme:

Old Dunmore's dead, that good old man;
Him we shall no more see.
He made these chimes to play themselves,
At twelve, nine, six and three.

The other major building of Hallaton is the early eighteenth-century Hallaton Hall, a distinguished grey-stone house. Privileged villagers live in terraces of stone cottages built between the seventeenth and nineteenth centuries.

On Easter Monday the villagers enjoy two quaint rituals. First, they share a hare pie, traditionally provided by the local rector. (In 1790 one rector, rightly suspecting that this was a pagan ritual, tried to end the tradition, to be greeted by the cry, 'No pie, no parson'.) Next, the villagers compete with nearby villages in 'bottle-kicking'. The 'bottles' are in fact casks of beer, which are pushed across a stream. Then the beer is drunk by villagers sitting atop Hallaton's unusually shaped, conical market cross. No doubt many of the players and spectators continue to celebrate in the village's three inns, *The Fox*, *The Royal Oak* and *The Bewicke Arms*.

The parish church of St. Michael and All Angels (opposite), *set above the village, combines the delicate Decorated tracery of its aisle windows with an impressive Norman tower and broach spire – an early example, for spires appeared on English churches only in the late twelfth century. Vignettes of Hallaton underline the exquisiteness of the village: flower arrangements in the church* (above left), *a Norman tympanum* (above), *and the combination of lane and cottage which is often at the heart of English village design* (left).

Southwell NOTTINGHAMSHIRE

*D*etails of the extraordinary carvings which decorate Southwell Minster *(above); the mighty church* (opposite) *was bequeathed to this village by the Normans. The pyramid roofs of two of the towers date from the earliest design of the church.*

THIS DELIGHTFUL SPOT is rendered extraordinary by its superb Minster or cathedral. Begun in the early twelfth century on the site of an earlier church, its nave and transepts still stand, the former supported by mighty Norman piers. The low central tower (with two more towers on the west face) was also built in the Norman style. In the aisles are Perpendicular windows – a style of architecture virtually confined to Britain – while the west window is a Perpendicular masterpiece.

A stone rood screen, carved around 1330 and sculpted with human heads, divides the nave from the exquisite Early English choir, which was begun in the twelve-thirties and finished in 1250. In the east window is Flemish stained-glass, brought here from the chapel of the Knights Templar in Paris. The brass lectern, which dates from around 1300, was recovered from the lake at Newstead Abbey, into which the monks flung it after the dissolution of their monastery at the time of the Reformation.

As if these glories were not enough for one ecclesiastical building, walk along the corridor which leads from the choir to the astounding octagonal chapter house. Nikolaus Pevsner has observed that polygonal chapter houses are an English speciality, but only at Southwell and York were the master masons bold enough to dispense with a central shaft to support the far-reaching ribs of the vault. York, however, has vaults of timber; only Southwell has a stone vault without a prop in the middle. But what makes the chapter house unique are the carvings – of oak, hawthorn, maple, ivy, hop and vine leaves and blossom.

The rest of Southwell (pronounced 'Suthell') is not to be neglected. South of the Minster is what remains of a late fourteenth-century palace. King Charles I stayed at the *Saracen's Head* in 1646, before surrendering to the Scots. And Byron and his mother lived in Georgian Burgage Manor, north of the village green.

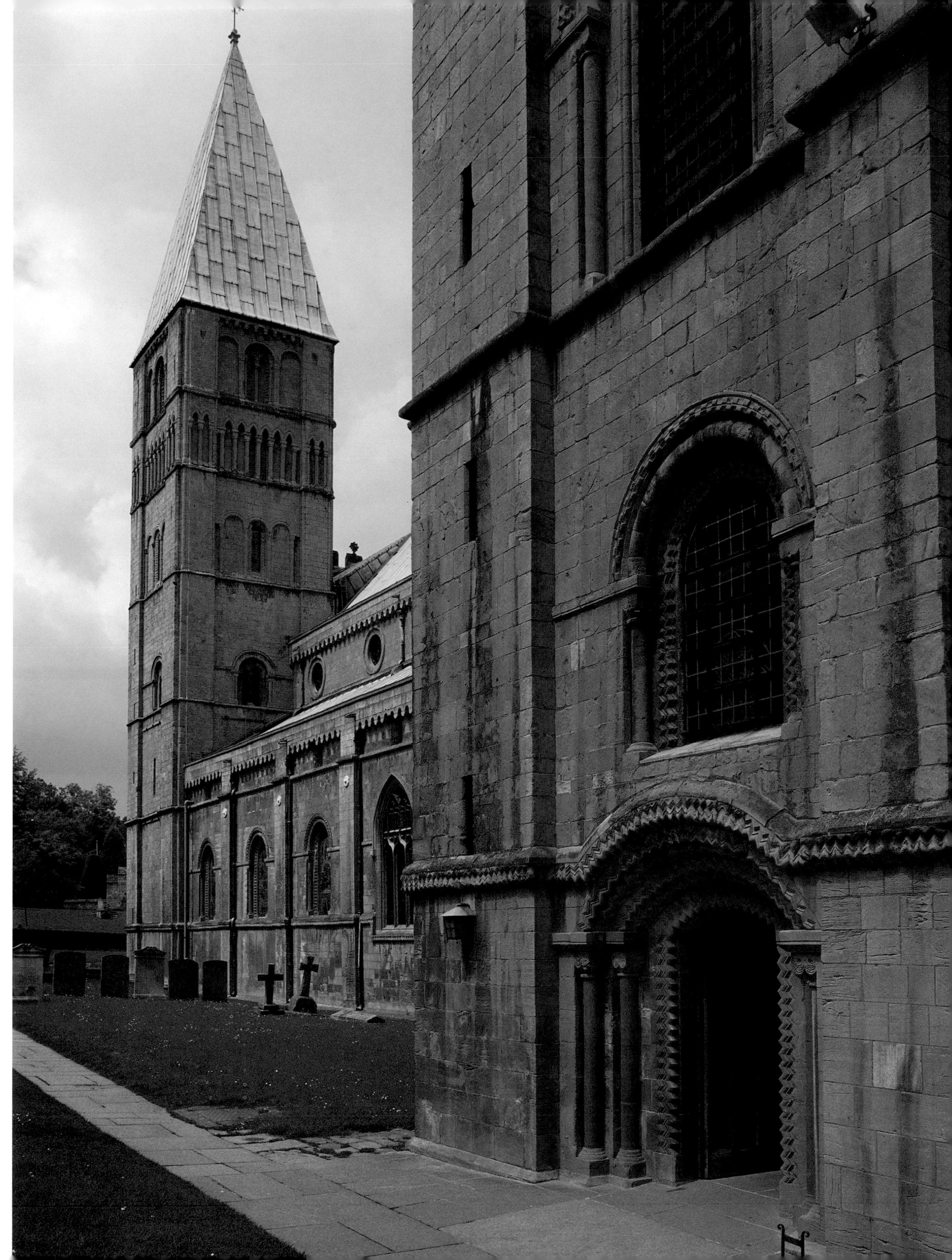

Both the ecclesiastical and secular buildings are unusually splendid for so small a place: the Saracen's Head (far right), *an inn made memorable by the despairing sojourn of King Charles I in 1646 at the end of the Civil War (the doors which guard its courtyard are some five hundred years old); a later inn* (right) *is the* Crown Hotel; *and Rampton Prebend* (above) *presents a pleasant face to Westgate.*

Some of the homelier aspects of this village are revealed on Queen Street (above) *and in daily business on King Street* (left *and* far left).

Welford-on-Avon

WARWICKSHIRE

A bend of the river Avon (above) *embraces the village on every side save the south. The river associations of the place are repeated in the name of Boat Lane* (opposite), *lined by dainty half-timbered houses.*

DELIGHTFULLY, the river Avon flows by three flanks of the outskirts of the Warwickshire village of Welford-on-Avon. Cross the river by its slender stone bridge and find yourself in the High Street. On one side is an idyllic village green. On both sides stand timber-framed and thatched cottages and houses, their gardens adding to the colourful charm of this village. North-east of the church of St. Peter stands Cleavers, a house built of brick in the mid Georgian era, comprising five bays, two storeys and decorated with stone quoins.

Enter the churchyard through its lych-gate. Look out for the plaque which remembers the former stocks and village pond. The church is mostly Romanesque (or, as the British put it, Norman) and Perpendicular in style. Its west tower is mostly Norman, as is the south doorway, under its typical zig-zag arch. The Normans declined to carve decorations on the north doorway, but inside they built fine arcades. The chancel is in the Decorated Gothic style, the pulpit Jacobean. And the whole church was sensitively restored in the eighteen-sixties by Sir Giles Gilbert Scott. Enjoy the delicious ambience of its situation in the village. Then refresh yourself in one of the village's pubs – *The Bell*, *The Shakespeare*, or *The Four Alls*.

Summer in an English village: the red, white and blue maypole of Welford-on-Avon is the focus of traditional dancing (left *and* above).

The tradition of timber-framed building goes back to the fifteenth century in Weobley (above *and* opposite). *A view of the village from the church tower shows that half-timbering can be a complex art; not a single house quite imitates its neighbour's design.*

Weobley HEREFORDSHIRE

AT WEOBLEY (which is pronounced 'Webley') the thirteenth-century parish church of St. Peter and St. Paul, with its lovely spire, scarcely predates *The Red Lion* inn, which has stood in this village since the fourteenth century. Some of the church's monuments date back to the Normans, though its finest treasure is a traceried, eight-sided font of the fourteenth century. Some of Weobley's black-and-white half-timbered houses overhang the streets, the finest of which is the wide central street with its rose garden. This is a village old enough to have been mentioned in the Domesday Book as 'Wibelai'.

Find south-west of Weobley The Ley. This timbered farmhouse, with its eight gables, was built in 1589. Those were times of religious persecution, and The Ley has a priest's hole in which Roman Catholic priests were hidden from their Protestant enemies. This exquisite village played its part in later strife, as the marble monument in the parish church to the regicide Colonel John Birch displays. (He eventually quarrelled with Oliver Cromwell, was imprisoned twenty-one times, and died in 1691.) This is border country, and well worth seeking out, twelve kilometres south-west of Weobley, is Kinnersley Castle, built to defend the border and in its present form dating from the sixteenth century.

Another fascinating feature of Weobley are the red-and-white Hereford beef cattle, first bred here in the late eighteenth century by a villager named Benjamin Tomkins.

PRIVATE
CAR PARK
HOTEL ENTRANCE

STUDIO
GALLERY
Tea Room
WINSOR & NEWTON'S
ARTISTS'
MATERIALS
PRIVATE HOTEL
PAINTINGS

The Red Lion (left) *dates from the fourteenth century; many of the ancient buildings of Weobley have upper storeys which overhang the street* (below).

The church of St. Peter and St. Paul (overleaf left) *houses this marble monument to John Birch, a commander of the Roundheads during the Civil War, who died in 1691. To the west of Weobley is the delightfully gabled, half-timbered farmhouse of 1589, known as The Ley* (overleaf right).

In Hope of Resurrection to Eternall Life
Here is Deposited the Body of
Coll IOHN BIRCH
(Descended of a Worthy Family in Lancashire)
As the Dignities He arrived at in the Field; and the
Esteem Universally yeilded him in the SENAT=HOUSE
Exceeded the Attainments of most; so they were but the
Moderate and Just Rewards of his Courage, Conduct-
Wisdom and Fidelity. None who new him denyed him, ye
Charatter of asserting & vindicating ye Laws & Liberties of
his Country in War, and of promoting its Welfare and
Prosperity in Peace; He was borne ye 7th of Sept. 1626
And died (a Member of ye Honble House of Comons
Being Burgess for Weobley)
May ye 10th 1691

The Eastern Counties

In London, John Constable, longing for his native Suffolk, wrote in praise of, 'The sound of water escaping from mill-dams, etc., willows, old rotten planks, slimy posts, and brickwork....' A tour through the villages of the eastern counties can indeed be immensely rewarding, not least because they retained a very separate identity until comparatively recently and also because of their delightful countryside and its waters, for this is undoubtedly watery country. Ditches drain Suffolk. Marshes and broads (around five thousand acres) water Norfolk.

The Humber estuary is the northern boundary of Lincolnshire, a county of water channels and flood banks. The villages here are mostly built of brick, many houses with attractive pantile roofs. Elsewhere, in a fenland of dykes, you may delight in churches built of local sandstone, though the villages which cluster round them are still mostly brick-built.

In Suffolk we enter a land of flint (with flint and freestone decoration known as flushwork), of limestone and of a grey stone called coralline-crag, and supremely of half-timbering – a skill with wood matched in the screens and benches of the churches. Another local speciality are the serpentine walls known as 'crinkle-crankles'. Travel along the coastal plain of Essex to find inland creeks. Cambridgeshire is in fen country, peat lands once infested with swamps. The Romans and then the Anglo-Saxons were among the first to set about draining the region. Thus, many of the villages described here are close to water. A stream flows through the Lincolnshire village of Castle Bytham, the Great Ouse washes the Cambridgeshire villages of Hemingford Grey and Hemingford Abbots; look out for perhaps the most famous village described in this book, Dedham in the valley of the river Stour.

As the many weavers' cottages in these villages reveal, this was wool country. Rich fifteenth-century clothiers built the church of Lavenham, whose Wool Hall now serves as an inn. Another wealthy wool merchant founded the magnificent church of Dedham, immortalized in the paintings of John Constable. Describing this part of England in 1821, William Cobbett criticized it as flat and wanting fine woods. Then he changed his mind and observed that this slice of England lacks nothing that Providence and the industry of man can give.

Famous in East Anglia are the so-called 'wool churches', such as fifteenth-century Dedham church (opposite), *Perpendicular in style, dedicated to St. Mary the Virgin, and paid for by a wool merchant named Thomas Webbe when the village was a centre of the wool trade; its magnificent tower rises some 131 feet.*

Eastern variety: a tract of Lincolnshire countryside, with a glimpse of the tower of the fourteenth-century church of St. Andrew at Folkingham, a village which sits on the edge of the fens (left)*; a corner of the half-timbered, Jacobean guild-hall of the Essex village of Thaxted, the open ground floor revealing that the building was once a market-hall* (top)*; the brick-built general store of the Norfolk village of Heydon* (above).

Castle Bytham

LINCOLNSHIRE

AT THE TIME of Domesday, the village was known as Westbitham; its name changed briefly to Great Bitham before becoming Castle Bytham. The first part of the present name refers to the Norman castle that stood here; Henry III had the main castle destroyed in 1221, but its earthworks still survive, divided from the village by a stream which flows into the river Glen. Bytham probably derives from Old English 'bytme', meaning 'wet valley bottom'.

The church of St. James, cruciform in pattern, is battlemented and has a lozenge frieze typical of this part of England. The top of the tower is Perpendicular Gothic in design. The rest of the church is earlier, much of it Decorated Gothic, notably the windows of the elongated chancel. A sculpture in the porch takes its origins back yet earlier, to Anglo-Saxon times.The east window has entrancing geometrical tracery. Do not miss the Easter Sepulchre in this chancel. Note also the tracery of the west window of the north aisle. Much of St. James's church is carved delightfully. Its transept is a nineteenth-century work, rebuilt in 1857. Inside, the church has preserved the brass candelabrum which used to light it in the nineteenth century, as well as a mid seventeenth-century octagonal font. Note its carvings, among them the letters *ihs* (representing Jesus) and the star of Bethlehem.

East of the church is the priory, in its present form a dignified seventeenth-century building, gabled and enhanced with lovely windows. Such fine windows also add their charm to the seventeenth-century, three-bayed Manor House in the high street.

The houses of Castle Bytham cluster around the lovely church of St. James, Decorated and Perpendicular Gothic in style (right).

Quaint cottages overlook the village duck-pond (left *and* below). *God's Acre, the old graveyard of Castle Bytham, surrounds its equally venerable parish church* (above).

Now, alas, a rare survivor in English villages, the carpenter's well-equipped workshop (above) *suggests a long tradition of country crafts at Castle Bytham.*

A luxuriant cottage garden adds joy and colour to Dedham (above). *Flatford Mill* (opposite) *was made famous by the paintings of John Constable; here lived his friend Willy Lott.*

Dedham ESSEX

THIS LOVELY VILLAGE in the valley of the river Stour has a church made famous by the paintings of John Constable. At Dedham he was educated at the Free Grammar School (with its delightful brickwork), which had been founded in 1732, forty-four years before his birth. A Latin inscription over a school door records the name of its first master, Thomas Grimwood. His son taught Constable Latin.

The battlemented church tower rises to a height of 131 feet. The village prospered from the wool trade in medieval times, and the church itself was founded by Thomas Webbe, a fifteenth-century wool merchant. His trademark is interspersed among the Tudor roses and portcullises carved on the passage through the tower. Look for the insignia of the Guild of Weavers and Millers, generous benefactors of this church, on the heraldic shields in the nave.

Southfields, a Tudor house, belonged to another wool merchant, and part of it also served as his factory. Sherman's is an elegant Georgian house, but derives its name from fifteenth-century wool merchants, ancestors of the American Civil War general, William T. Sherman. But if you look above the shop fronts in Dedham's High Street you discover more attractive storeys of brick and plaster. The same street is also notable for a couple of inns: *The Sun* (note its coaching archway) and *The Marlborough Head* (once the home and workshop of medieval clothiers and dyers).

Another celebrated artist, Sir Alfred Munnings, became famous in the twentieth century for his paintings of horses, and much of his work is found in his former home here, Castle House, south of the village. Flatford Mill, which belonged to Constable's father and where the artist worked for a while, is close by, south-east of Dedham. The painting of Willy Lott's cottage in Flatford is one of Constable's most famous. The river Stour also flows through here, lined by willow and ash as it winds through the Essex countryside.

There is tranquillity and diversity in this Essex village; a number of large elegant houses hint at its traditional prosperity (this page).

Like many an English village, Dedham displays an incredible variety of architectural styles and building materials (this page).

PLEASE DO NOT
FISH FROM THE
CHURCHYARD.

This notice outside the parish church of Hemingford Grey seems slightly incongruous (opposite), *since the church preaches the gospel of one who urged his disciples to be fishers of men! Presumably the cat sitting happily on a tomb in the churchyard would ignore the notice if presented with something from the river for lunch.*

Hemingford Grey

CAMBRIDGESHIRE

HEMINGFORD GREY and its sister village, Hemingford Abbots, occupy a delightful position on a fordable, willow-shaded bend of the Great Ouse river. House-boats and cruisers tie up beside the river bank. At Hemingford Grey the river also provided the power for a water-mill. The moated manor house there, built around 1130 and standing south-west of the church, has diapered brickwork, as well as Norman windows (round-headed) and a Norman doorway. Timbered, often built of mellow brick and thatched, the houses are enchanting. Among them, Glebe Cottage dates from 1583, and Hemingford Grey House was built in the seventeenth century. Beautifully sited close by the river, the twelfth-century church of St. James boasted a spire until 1741, when a gale toppled it. Local lore holds that its remnants lie in the river itself.

The parish church of St. Margaret, Hemingford Abbots, was built of brown cobbles around 1300; no-one should miss its majestic spire and, inside, angels and other figures depicted playing musical instruments in the roof of the church.

A lych-gate opens the way to the churchyard and the church of St. Margaret, Hemingford Abbots, surmounted by its elegant spire (opposite). *The half-timbered and whitewashed cottages of the same village seem almost to have grown from the fields of Cambridgeshire* (this page).

Heydon NORFOLK

AGAINST THE NORTH WALL of the chancel of Heydon's parish church of St. Peter and St. Paul is a mortuary chapel. More uplifting is its west tower, clad in knapped flint and dating from the mid fifteenth century. The double-storeyed south porch is Perpendicular in style and its vault has charming bosses. Perpendicular windows also light the aisles and chancel, with some Decorated Gothic stonework enlivening the west windows.

Here, too, is a thirteenth-century font. The pulpit mirrors the Perpendicular style of most of the church; the screen dates from 1480; pews once owned by individual families can still be inspected here. The north aisle boasts a string of tombs. Yet in spite of these, this is a curiously uplifting house of God, sited alongside an exquisite Norfolk village green. Among the houses is one said to be the former bakery of Heydon Hall.

The Hall itself dates from the early fifteen-eighties. Built for an auditor of the Exchequer named Henry Dynne, it has interestingly irregular windows, with mullions and transoms. A couple of rows of polygonal chimneys rise above the roof. There are also seventeenth- and eighteenth-century fireplaces.

Do not miss Cropton Hall, a mile or so north-west of Heydon. The west front was created at the beginning of the eighteenth century (or maybe a trifle earlier). Note the Doric pilasters, made of brick. Once again, the gables typical of this part of England play a prominent part in the design.

This peaceful Norfolk village green is laid out on the south side of Heydon's splendid parish church, which is discreetly battlemented and embellished with a staircase tower, (the extension housing the staircase is clearly visible in this photograph) (right).

Inside the parish church of St. Peter and St. Paul (opposite) *all is architecturally harmonious, with a Perpendicular style pulpit (with a sounding board) and a screen in the same style. Note the curly Jacobean altar rails in the side chapel and the piscina in the wall on the right. Note, too, the poppy-head pew ends and the diamond-shaped hatchment on the wall of the chancel.*

Outside, the village is as striking as its church (above *and* above left), *with its well, Georgian doorways and a forge distinguished by the figures of a horse and foal made from horseshoes* (left). *The many-gabled Heydon Hall and the High Street* (overleaf) *add notes of architectural distinction.*

W
E

Free House

Lavenham SUFFOLK

SOME OF the finest English clerestories (the upper storeys of nave walls in churches) are pierced by Perpendicular windows, and the greatest can be found in the eastern part of the country. That of the church of St. Peter and St. Paul, rising on its hill above Lavenham in Suffolk, is equal to any, if it is not the greatest of all. Wealthy clothiers built this church after 1485, rejoicing at the end of the Wars of the Roses. Before entering the church, look for the coats of arms of two of these clothiers, the Earl of Oxford and Thomas Spryng, on the church's majestic tower.

Note the boar, emblem of the Oxford family, on the south porch. Thomas Spryng spared nothing to ensure the future life of himself and his family. Inside the church an inscription on the Spryng Chapel begs visitors to pray for his own soul and that of his wife. On a monumental brass in the vestry, the parents and their children are depicted rising from their shrouds. The early sixteenth-century chantry chapels are sumptuously carved; the rood screen of St. Peter and St. Paul, though, was carved earlier, in the fourteenth century. The choir-stalls have delightful misericords.

This church is surrounded by a lovely village; its streets of half-timbered houses encompass the market-place (with its early sixteenth-century cross, where bears were once tied to be baited, and the half-timbered guild-hall of 1529). There are also Tudor shops and the Wool Hall (now transformed into the *Swan Hotel*). Look out for craft symbols of clothiers in the plasterwork of weavers' cottages. Without the river, of course, wool and this village and its splendid church could never have flourished.

Rising on a hill above the village, finished around 1520, built throughout of flushwork, Lavenham church (right) *ranks among the greatest of the Suffolk 'wool churches'. It was endowed in part by a clothier who begged forgiveness from Henry VII for occasionally cheating his customers; its magnificent tower rises to a height of 141 feet.*

HALL ROAD
LEADING TO PARK ROAD

This East Anglian village prospered from the cloth trade during the Middle Ages, and the rich decor of its houses (left) *testifies to its traditional wealth. Shilling Street* (above) *derives its name from a Flemish weaver named Schyling, one of several who came here to impart their skills to local artisans. One of Lavenham's finest fifteenth-century half-timbered buildings is Little Hall* (top).

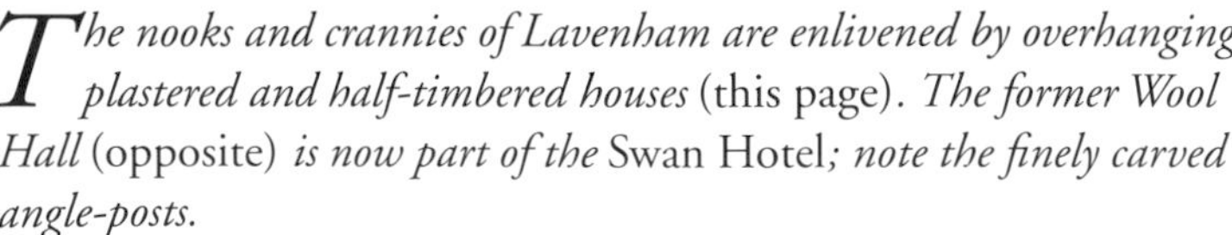

The nooks and crannies of Lavenham are enlivened by overhanging, plastered and half-timbered houses (this page). *The former Wool Hall* (opposite) *is now part of the* Swan Hotel; *note the finely carved angle-posts.*

Changes of texture and colour in Lavenham: the garden of Little Hall provides a glimpse of traditional cultivation (below)*; a half-timbered, gabled house contrasts with an eighteenth-century pargeted house with a charming fanlight, yet the two sit quite harmoniously together* (right).

The Southern Counties

THAT ST. MICHAEL'S CHURCH at Amberley in Sussex stands on land given by a Saxon king in the late seventh century indicates the antiquity of the villages of the southern part of England. Aldbury in Hertfordshire is in origin even older than Amberley. The Hampshire village of Wherwell grew up around a late tenth-century nunnery. The Kentish village of Elham is probably equally old, though its present church dates only from the twelfth century. Windsor, across the river Thames from the exquisite village of Eton, with its overwhelming college, has a castle begun by the Normans.

Here we touch on the Royal County of Berkshire, a landscape replete with materials for brick buildings but with little stone (hence the decision to build Eton College chapel in expensive stone, to emphasize its importance, while the rest of the college is mostly brick). Another county in this mild region is Buckinghamshire, river-crossed and part of the chalk belt of England known as the Chilterns. Here in the Thames valley is one of England's magically preserved villages, Nether Winchendon, with its manor house and superb church.

The rivers Wey and Mole drain Surrey into the Thames. Much of that county, though so near to London, has remained remarkably pastoral. These are counties celebrated by many a generation of English writers; Hilaire Belloc described one of them as, '...that part of England which is very properly called her Eden, that centre of all good things and home of happy men, the county of Sussex.'

This old well and parish pump (opposite) *in Surrey at Leigh (pronounced 'Lye') are potent reminders of village life in times gone by.*

30

Thames-side Cookham, here enjoying its fair (left), *is famed for its connection with the painter Stanley Spencer, while Leigh* (top) *and Amberley* (above), *respectively of Surrey and Sussex, show just how charming the most beautiful villages of southern England can be.*

Aldbury
HERTFORDSHIRE

ALDBURY is Anglo-Saxon for 'old fort'. If this spot, set on the border of the Chilterns, was old in Anglo-Saxon times, then it is truly venerable. Today it centres beguilingly on a triangular village green and a pond where the villagers' ducks swim placidly. Reminders of less peaceful activities are the whipping-post and stocks for the punishment of miscreants.

Close by the green rises the church of St. John the Baptist. Its tower is faced with flint. In part this church dates from the thirteenth century. Inside, find the Pendley Chapel, which shelters the late-medieval tomb and effigies of Sir Robert Whittingham and his wife. The church's wooden lectern dates from the sixteenth century.

Aldbury is a *mélange* of cottages, some brick and tile, others timber-framed, most of them built in the sixteenth and seventeenth centuries. The village once deployed a communal bread-oven, still recognizable by its unusually tall chimney. In contrast with this humbly delightful part of the village is an urn set on a Greek Doric column above the beech trees of Ashbridge Park. It was set up in 1832 in memory of Francis Egerton, third Duke of Bridgewater, who was known as the Canal Duke, since he employed Joseph Brindley to construct the first canal in England – an engineering miracle which eventually stretched for sixty-seven-and-a-half kilometres. The 172 steps up to the Bridgewater Monument are well worth climbing for the magnificent views.

Just outside the village is the eighteenth-century Stocks House, once the home of the Victorian novelist Mrs Humphry Ward. And not far away another delight is the Georgian Gothic Ashridge House, which James Wyatt began building in 1808 and finished in 1814. It sits in a park designed by Humphry Repton and 'Capability' Brown.

Aldbury's duck-pond on the village green (below) *reflects two magical half-timbered houses. Note beside the pond the stocks, which were last used, it is said, to discipline a drunkard. This half-timbered and gabled house* (opposite) *is another example of delightful architecture in a village where almost every dwelling is a gem of the builder's art.*

ANDERSON
The LADY
Underneath are Interrd the Bodyes of Sr RICHARD
in the COUNTY of HERTFORD BART & DAME
was one of the Sisters and Coheirs of the Right
LORD VISCOUNT HEWYT BARON of GORAN in
of IRELAND.
also are Interrd their two Sons HENRY and
without Issue, and their Sole Daughter
HARCOURT Esqr by whom she had
two Sons HENRY and RICHARD, and three
and ARABELLA The rest sleep
and expectation of a joyfull
Veni cito Domine Jesu

The Gothic parclose screen (left) *of the Pendley Chapel of Aldbury parish church dates from 1575 and encloses the late-medieval tomb and effigies of Sir Robert Whittingham and his wife. Continuity of life could be the theme of the two photographs* (above), *from the churchyard of St. Peter and St. Paul to the village children seen against the backdrop of the church tower.*

Aldbury's post office (above), *as in many an English village, also serves as the village store.* The Greyhound *inn* (above right) *has a sign which inventively includes a detail from Paolo Uccello's* Hunt in the Forest. *A group of cottages* (right), *including a number thatched and half-timbered, and* (opposite) *this view of houses overlooking the village pond underline the architectural opulence of Aldbury.*

NO PARKING

Bloodstock from the stables of Aldbury pass by the village green (above). *A general view of the village shows how the parish church, as often happens in English villages, stands slightly apart from the main concentration of houses* (right).

Amberley SUSSEX

THIS EXTRAORDINARY VILLAGE seems completely unplanned, its streets run so haphazardly. Each of its houses is a unique construction – some made of stone, others of brick or flint, some thatched, others tiled (sometimes stone-tiled). It lies on the prehistoric South Downs Way, protected by a massive hill. Close by are thirty square miles of grazing land known as Amberley Wild Brooks (the word 'wild' deriving from Weald), which were celebrated in a piano piece by the composer John Ireland.

In the past the village was also protected by Amberley Castle, today for the most part in ruins. Overlooking the river Arun, this fortress was the summer home of the Bishops of Chichester, begun after the Norman Conquest by Bishop Luffa and continually extended throughout the Middle Ages. Battlemented, with a ruined gatehouse, its walls preserve intact a manor house.

In 681 a Saxon king, converted to Christianity by St. Wilfrid, gave the saint the land on which stands St. Michael's church. In its present form it dates mostly from the Norman Conquest and, like the castle, derived much from the patronage of Bishop Luffa. It shelters wall-paintings of the Resurrection and of Christ in Majesty. A medieval brass monument depicts a knight in armour and a surcoat. The tower holds a peal of five bells. In a former lime-works local history is set out in the Amberley Chalk Pits Museum.

The haphazard, yet entrancing village of Amberley (above), *is surrounded by equally beautiful countryside* (opposite).

A venerable porch graces one of Amberley's larger houses (opposite)*. Inside the twelfth- and thirteenth-century church of St. Michael, the chancel, with its fretted ceiling, is separated from the nave by a Norman arch* (below *and* right). *And here is a fifteenth-century monumental brass effigy of a former worshipper, a knight who now sleeps in peace* (below right).

A village street winds downhill, flanked by houses of diverse styles with traditional front gardens, more examples of the architectural eclecticism of the English village (these pages).

Elham KENT

NOT FAR from the Kent coast, set on chalk downlands, Elham is centred on a little square north of the church. In 1251 a charter was granted by the future monarch Edward I for Elham to hold a market in this square. Today a couple of inns flank it: the sixteenth-century coaching-inn named *The Rose and Crown* and the medieval *King's Arms.*

Explore the overhanging timber-framed, brick-and-tile village houses which date back to the Middle Ages, as well as eighteenth-century red-brick buildings. Particularly entrancing are those in the curving High Street. The finest is *The Abbot's Fireside* inn, rebuilt in 1614, timbered, its upper storey resting on carved brackets. Here Wellington lived during the Napoleonic wars. At the end of the High Street is a Methodist chapel built in 1839. Explore also the parallel Row Lane, where stands a medieval hall (today Well Cottage and Uptown Cottage), as well the seventeenth-century timbered Old Manor House.

The parish church of St. Mary the Virgin is a treat. Its twelfth-century north door is decorated with a seventeenth-century wooden hood mould and a brick gable. Part of its nave also dates from the twelfth century. In this nave are scripture sentences painted in the seventeenth century. The chancel was built in the thirteenth century, its tower in the late fourteenth century.

F. C. Eden, an underestimated twentieth-century architect, sensitively restored this church. His is the organ loft of 1911. He created the south aisle west window in 1915. And another of the treasures among its stained-glass, part of which dates back to the fifteenth century, is one in which you can recognize William Gladstone, Thomas Carlyle, Benjamin Disraeli, three of Queen Victoria's daughters and other worthies. Look out also for the fifteenth-century alabaster triptych.

Sitting in the Nailbourne valley in the chalk downlands of Kent, Elham is surrounded by famously lush countryside, a richness continued in the glorious planting along its main street (right).

The spire of the parish church of St. Mary the Virgin just edges over one of the old clapboard houses of the village (above right). *By contrast,* The Abbot's Fireside *inn* (below right) – *medieval, though in part rebuilt in 1614 – is one of the village's most significant half-timbered houses, while* above *and* opposite *are houses of quite different styles.*

The furnishings of Elham's parish church (left) *are exquisite and mostly twentieth-century, due to the superb restoration work of the architect F.C. Eden. The church dominates this community* (opposite)*; begun in the twelfth century and built of flint and ragstone, its spire rises high above the finely detailed houses of this beautiful Kent village* (below).

Beyond the corner of the half-timbered Moot Hall is revealed the parish church of Elstow (above), *which once served a long-disappeared Norman abbey. Once again, half-timbered, overhanging cottages* (right) *display the great charm of this style of vernacular architecture.*

Elstow

BEDFORDSHIRE

ITS ASSOCIATION with John Bunyan gives Elstow added interest. Born here in 1628, the son of a tinker whose trade he followed, he was baptized in the parish church. After service as a Parliamentarian soldier in the Civil War, he came back in 1645 and four years later married an impoverished girl of the village, whose two books (*The Plain Man's Pathway to Heaven* and *The Practice of Piety*) inspired his own writings.

Here you can find the cottage in which he lived. His followers used to meet in the fifteenth-century timber-and-brick Moot Hall on the village green. It now houses some of his few remains as well as a museum of life in the seventeenth century. He was wrestling and playing tip-cat on the village green when a voice from heaven inspired him to a radical change of life ('Wilt thou leave thy sins and go to Heaven, or have thy sins and go to Hell?'). Bunyan used to ring the bells in the detached belfry of the parish church (though later scruples led him to abandon the practice). This church, dedicated to St. Mary and St. Helena, is a splendid building – much of it thirteenth-century – which once served as the chapel of a Norman abbey for women.

The ruins of Houghton House near Ampthill to the south of Elstow ('House Beautiful' in The Pilgrim's Progress*)* (above)*; a wooden statue of John Bunyan is in Elstow church* (right), *as is the octagonal font* (far right) *in which he, his family (and of course many others) were baptized. Mementoes of John Bunyan and of life in the seventeenth century are displayed in the Moot Hall* (opposite).

*E*ton College chapel *(opposite above left)* graces this foundation which dates from 1440 and the charitable instincts of King Henry VI. A mock-Tudor arch *(opposite above right)* leads into Weston's Yard, where an oval lawn delights those privileged to live there. A pupil, in the quaint garb of the school, trudges through the village *(opposite below)*.

Eton BERKSHIRE

BASICALLY, Eton consists of a street and a college. At the end of Eton High Street a hump-backed bridge, not open to traffic, spans the river Thames, on which swans serenely float. Beyond Eton Bridge rises Windsor, a Victorian town, apart from its majestic castle, begun by the Normans and inhabited since then by the sovereigns of Britain and members of their families, as well as their servants. Here, too, is a guild-hall, finished by Sir Christopher Wren in 1689.

Eton College occupies the opposite end of Eton High Street. Founded by Henry VI in 1440, most of its buildings are in red brick, but the Perpendicular chapel, once the most important building of the college, is in grey and white stone. It was never finished. On a wall in the street, opposite the chapel's west end, a plaque marks the spot to which its nave should have extended. Inside the chapel is modern stained-glass, the west window of 1952 (depicting the Crucifixion) by Evie Hone, and side windows by John Piper illustrating some of Jesus's parables and miracles. The fan vaulting of 1958 by Sir William Holford is a disappointment, but the wall-paintings of 1479 to 1488 are remarkable.

Two quadrangles (known as 'yards') comprise the main school. Other pupils live in houses spread on either side of the High Street and surrounding streets. Watching Eton boys playing cricket in summer, some remember the words of Thomas Gray's *Ode on a Distant Prospect of Eton College*:

Alas! regardless of their doom,
The little victims play!
No sense have they of ills to come,
Nor care beyond to-day.

Leave Eton to discover Maidenhead, situated on an entrancing stretch of the Thames lined with elegant riverside hotels.

*S*wans gather beside Eton Bridge *(above left)* which spans the Thames; and a flowery corner of this delectable spot retains its privacy, despite the many visitors *(above)*.

Nether Winchendon

BUCKINGHAMSHIRE

Nether Winchendon House (above), *in origin a medieval stone construction with angle towers, was delightfully 'Gothicized' towards the end of the eighteenth century. Three of the towers still stand, as well as some circular brick chimneys. The village has other fine houses; this particularly attractive one* (opposite) *stands next to the church of St. Nicholas.*

WHEREAS many a church dominates its village, that of St. Nicholas at Nether Winchendon lies below a steep hill. Though the building is medieval, its interior is decked out in seventeenth- and eighteenth-century fashion: a Jacobean pulpit, retaining its tester or sounding board; hatchments; box pews; scripture sentences. Here are fifteenth-century monumental brasses, as well as fifteenth- and sixteenth-century stained-glass windows. Some of the glass in the south windows is Flemish. The chancel was rebuilt in 1891, though the arch remains from the era of Decorated Gothic architecture.

Walk west of the church to find on the door of the half-timbered Manor Farm the date 1620 inscribed over a door. Other fine, though lesser Nether Winchendon houses are also half-timbered, the timbers filled in with brick. Nether Winchendon House, however, outshines the rest. Early Tudor in style, it boasts circular, ornamented chimneys and angle towers. The great hall has an early seventeenth-century fireplace, with a triple-arched screen. The south-east room is deliciously decorated in the Early Renaissance style, with such features as a mermaid and foliage. Linen-fold panels also enhance this room.

The late eighteenth-century owners of Nether Winchendon House decided to give it a Gothic aspect, adding new battlements and a couple of Gothic windows.

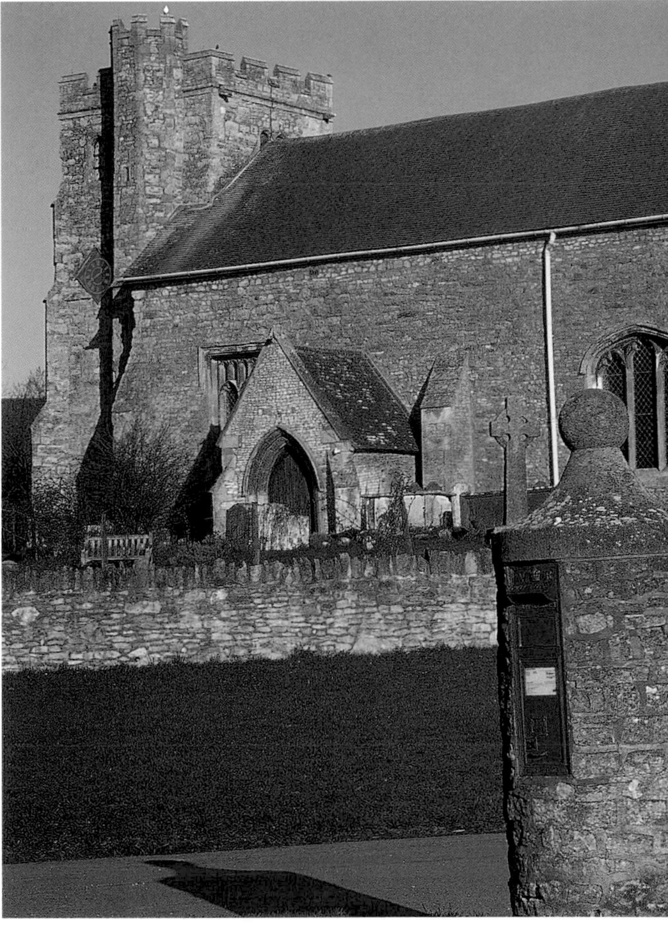

The parish church of Nether Winchendon (left and above) *has a solid foursquare look; it dates originally from the Middle Ages, but was substantially refurbished and rebuilt in subsequent centuries.*

Ockley SURREY

IN 851 the Danes invaded England. At Ockley in Surrey the English, led by Ethelwulf, ruler of Wessex, took them on in battle and after an immense struggle defeated them. Then the English massacred the surviving Danes. According to the chroniclers, the blood, possibly on the village green, flowed ankle-deep.

The long green survives to this day, an irregular swathe at times some two hundred metres wide, elsewhere a mere fifty metres. Today it is lined by delightful brick-and-tile houses. These include, on the west side, a couple known as Carpoles Cottages, and at the south end The Tuns, with an eighteenth-century weather-boarded front, and the haphazard Tanyard Cottages built of brick and timber-framed. On the north side of the green are the rough-cast Lime Tree Cottages, tile-hung like the rest.

The parish church, dedicated to St. Margaret, rises north-east of the village. Its wooden porch dates from the fifteenth century, the west tower from 1699. An east window in the nave preserves Decorated tracery. The church was comprehensively restored in 1873, from which year dates most of its furniture, including the rood screen. Another charming feature of Ockley, opposite the church, is the mid eighteenth-century Ockley Court, a fine three-storeyed brick building. Beyond Ockley rises Leith Hill (where some historians allege that the famous battle took place and not on the village green, for here human remains were excavated in 1882).

Essential flavours of a Surrey village: the fine wooden porch of St. Margaret's church (opposite), *the cricket field* (above), *and brick-and-tile houses* (right).

Wherwell
HAMPSHIRE

WHERWELL lies cool and sweet beside the river Test, its main street lined with thatched, black-and-white cottages. The thatch is often sumptuous, sweeping down over eaves and windows, stretching towards the ground, and sometimes even covering walls. Gavel Acre, the Old Malt House and Aldings offer three splendid examples of this craft.

The river Test once flowed by a nunnery, founded in 986 by Queen Elfrida (the mother of Ethelred the Unready) as an expiation for the death of her stepson, King Edward the Martyr, whom she murdered at Corfe Castle in 978.

Today all that remains is the church of St. Peter and the Holy Cross, reached by a bridge over the river; this church was in fact rebuilt in the nineteenth century – though by a skilled Gothic Revival architect named Henry Woodyer. Wooden tiles protect its tower. A semi-circular turret reveals stairs. One genuine survival of the priory is the tombstone of a fourteenth-century abbess set inside in its wall. And there are some Saxon and medieval sculptures also preserved inside. Note especially the early fourteenth-century *Noli me tangere* and a Harrowing of Hell. Note, too, the carving of a nun on an early fifteenth-century tomb, as well as the tomb of Sir Owen West, who died in 1551, and the Victorian mausoleum of the Iremongers.

Henry VIII had the priory destroyed during the Dissolution of the Monasteries, and today a fine early nineteenth-century house on the spot has usurped the name of The Priory. This Priory has a cupola, a porch in the Tuscan Renaissance style and a dining-room whose magnificent ceiling is coved.

Wherwell is notable for cottages thatched in deep brown straw (opposite *and* above).

The master thatcher has a difficult and vital task in this Hampshire village, shaping his new work in the age-old fashion (above, above right *and* opposite). *The village church* (right), *rebuilt in the nineteenth century, which is approached by crossing a little bridge spanning the river, is dedicated to St. Peter and the Holy Cross. As is often observed, its belfry seems like another church perched on top of the original.*

Along the Test valley from Wherwell a fine old mill-house looks out over the water – a scene made even more magical by a weeping willow.

The Western Counties

MONASTERIES AND ABBEYS have left us a priceless legacy in the western counties of England. At Dunster in Somerset the legacy is both Benedictine and Cistercian, the former giving us the parish church as well as other splendid monastic buildings, the latter bequeathing a guest house which is now a public house. Remains of a Benedictine abbey also survive at Cerne Abbas in Dorset. And Lacock Abbey in Wiltshire, founded in 1232, though long secularized, has retained an astonishing group of monastic buildings.

The south-west peninsula of England has always seemed somehow more intimate with the sea than other parts of the English coast. Mevagissey, for instance, offers diversely delightful seaside environments. Clovelly's quay dates from the fourteenth century. Its whitewashed houses were restored in the early twentieth century by Christine Hamlyn, mistress of eighteenth-century Clovelly Court. By contrast, Mevagissey has a double harbour, houses with slate- and plank-clad walls and an eighteenth-century boat-builders' shed.

Curiously, some parts of Somerset lie below sea-level. Other parts of this delectable region, Dartmoor in particular, rise almost as high as the Peak District in Derbyshire. But here one especially remembers and agrees with William Thackeray's astute observation of the gentleness of the English landscape that, 'it seems to shake hands with you as you pass through it.' And, as you feast on clotted cream in the West Country, Leigh Hunt's delight some hundred and fifty years ago in the pastoral scenery of this part of England still rings true: traversing it, it seemed to him, 'like a breakfast of milk and cream.'

A signpost directs visitors to the Devonshire village of Clovelly (opposite). *Once a neglected backwater, Clovelly was transformed by its squire, George Cary, an entrepreneur who in his will of 1601 declared, 'I have of late created a pier or key* [sic] *in the sea or river of the Severne upon the sea-shore, near low water of the said seas.' Thus a few scattered cottages and farms became a picturesque fishing port, now preserved from motorized traffic.*

CLOVELLY
NO VEHICULAR
ACCESS

Quintessential West Country: a thatched cottage at Cockington (top) *and a modest house front at Mevagissey* (above)*; the ruins of Norman Corfe Castle rise like a jagged tooth over the village* (right).

Cerne Abbas

DORSET

CERNE ABBAS is famed above all for the priapic figure of a naked man, holding a huge, knobbed club, all of which some 1500 years ago was cut into the turf of a chalk hillside north-east of the village. Some have speculated that he is an English version of Hercules; 180 feet tall, this effigy may well have been connected with ancient fertility rites. Certainly some two hundred years ago women were still sleeping on the hillside in the belief that proximity to the figure would cure their barrenness.

Above the Cerne Abbas giant you can make out the traces of a rectangular earthwork fortress. In the village itself stand remnants of a former Benedictine abbey founded in the tenth century: part of its fourteenth-century tithe barn; the impressive fifteenth-century, three-storeyed, mullioned gatehouse; and the guest house.

But, as in many such villages, the parish church of St. Mary remains an impressive survivor, with a late Norman chancel, a pre-Reformation Madonna, heraldic glass and a fifteenth-century buttressed tower. Its wall-paintings in the chancel date from the fourteenth century, its screen from the fifteenth. The pulpit, with its tester, is seventeenth-century, and the east window almost certainly came from the abbey church – and one can see how it was reduced in size to slot into its present position. The churchyard contains a wishing-well, said (erroneously) to have been blessed by St. Augustine, and from this well water flows down to the duck-pond by the village green.

Cerne Abbas has thatched cottages in Long Street, and Tudor houses in Abbey Street, one of the most impressive of which is the gabled Abbey Farm, constructed of flint and stone.

This village's most famous sight is its priapic giant, sculpted in the turf of a neighbouring hill some one-and-a-half millennia ago (opposite). *Cerne Abbas itself is a delightful place of widely differing architectural styles.*

The old abbey grounds, the Royal Oak *inn, and the fifteenth-century tower of the church of St. Mary* (this page) *make this one of the most attractive villages of the West Country. The church dominates the picturesque houses which are gathered in this delightfully wooded spot* (opposite).

Clovelly DEVON

THIS MUST SURELY be the loveliest of all Devon villages. Traffic-free, it has a main street that rises from the pebbled beach, the minuscule fishing harbour and the old stone jetty which curves delightfully and has an inn, fortunately, since the climb up the street is steep and long. Flanked by often whitewashed cottages of diverse styles, in half a mile this main street rises four hundred feet. High, wooded cliffs rise around the village.

A line of yew trees leads to the parish church of All Saints, which stands on top of the cliff. It has a Norman porch with dog-tooth decoration and a Jacobean pulpit. Its tower is early medieval. The font is Norman, the aisle Perpendicular, the wagon roof splendid. The father of the nineteenth-century novelist Charles Kingsley was once rector here, and the church has a monument to the novelist, as well as many other memorials. That to Sir Robert Cary in the chancel recalls a man who attended Exeter Assizes in 1586 and fatally contracted gaol fever. Look out also for the seats specially reserved for the children of pauper families, who were forbidden to sit with other young people. Note the colours of the east window, created by Kempe in 1885, and that by Sir Ninian Comper in 1905 which depicts the Annunciation. Next to the church stands Clovelly Court, rebuilt in the Georgian era, but retaining a fourteenth-century wing.

The most entrancing way of reaching Clovelly is by Hobby Drive, east of the village, which winds for some three miles along tree-bedecked cliffs. Near Clovelly is an Iron Age hill-fortress, Clovelly Dykes, comprising three concentric banks separated by ditches.

An Elizabethan squire created this fishing village, whose steep streets and exquisite houses today attract countless visitors (left *and* opposite). *A series of cobbled terraces (where once flowed a stream which was eventually diverted) run down to the harbour.*

Clovelly's curved stone pier (left) *now shelters small pleasure craft. Whitewashed houses, decked out with flowers and all with magnificent views, perch above the sea* (top *and* above).

HOTEL
OH
1928
BD278

*T*he Red Lion Hotel *looks out over the harbour from its vantage point on the venerable containing wall* (opposite).

The streets and alleys of the village are replete with tranquil enclaves (this page), *in spite of the many visitors.*

The Devonshire countryside (overleaf) *has delightful corners of ancient building and deep lanes bordered by high, thick hedges, which bespeak centuries of settlement.*

Dunster SOMERSET

NORMAN INVADERS built Dunster's first castle. In subsequent years its successor, rebuilt in the fourteenth century, witnessed stirring times, not least during the Civil War, when Royalists valiantly defended the battlemented fortress before eventually surrendering in 1646 to the Roundheads. Much was then destroyed, but with the Restoration of the monarchy came a restoration of Dunster Castle, now enhanced by a magnificent oak and elm staircase, carved with hunting scenes, and a superb plaster ceiling in the dining room. The chapel was added in the eighteenth century and a couple more towers in the nineteenth. At the opposite end of the High Street stands another eighteenth-century building, a folly of 1775.

Initially, Dunster's parish church of St. George served both Benedictine monks and the villagers, their respective space divided by a breathtakingly carved, fan-vaulted rood screen, fifty-four feet long and stretching across the nave and the aisles. From the twelfth century remains the church's west door, while the chancel dates from the next century. Most of the rest was built in the fifteenth century.

The monks have long gone from Dunster, but their former priory, their circular dovecote (with its revolving ladder) and their tithe barn remain in this entrancing village; so does their fourteenth-century guest house – three-storeyed, slate-hung and today called The Nunnery.

Another monastic foundation, first built in the fifteenth century and in part rebuilt in the second decade of the sixteenth century, was the Cistercian guest house which now serves as *The Luttrell Arms*. Its ceiling is vaulted and hammer-beamed. But the most unusual feature of Dunster is its octagonal Yarn Market. Built in the seventeenth century, it served merchants who came to buy the local cloth, known as 'Dunsters'.

The majestic parish church of Dunster (opposite) *once served a Benedictine priory. Begun in the twelfth century, its present form is basically fifteenth-century. The exceptionally long rood screen* (above) *has fourteen bays.*

Dunster Castle, built by the Norman Baron de Mohun four years after William the Bastard conquered England, dominates a village whose delightful features include the seventeenth-century Yarn Market, seen here in the foreground.

The diversity of a Somerset village (these pages)*: Dunster's streets are flanked by quaint houses, an inn and a peaceful churchyard.*

This cranny of the village (above) *is created by old stone and the weathered patterns of a half-timbered house, whose structure clearly differs considerably from that* opposite*; another charming example of the wide range of English vernacular architecture.*

Lacock WILTSHIRE

THE CURVING STREETS of Lacock are flanked by whitewashed, half-timbered cottages and houses built out of warm grey stone, not one of which was constructed later than the eighteenth century. Many, indeed, are medieval. Some lean out over the streets; others are gabled, such as Porch House in the High Street. *The Red Lion Hotel* was built in the eighteenth century, while in East Street can be seen a fourteenth-century barn.

Two ecclesiastical buildings add more to this lovely village. The mainly fifteenth-century parish church of St. Cyriac is Perpendicular in style; its east window is especially magnificent, as are its splendid aisles.

Lacock Abbey, which had been the home of Augustinian canonesses since its foundation by Ela, Countess of Salisbury, in 1232, was dissolved at the Reformation but nonetheless retains the nuns' chapter house, the sacristy, the warming room, the kitchen, the lavatory and thirteenth-century cloisters. In the mid sixteenth century its new owner, Sir William Sharington, set about converting the abbey into a stately home, and it was he who commissioned the octagonal tower which overlooks the river Avon. The Gothic hall and dining room on the west side were added in the seventeen-fifties. In the early nineteenth century Lacock Abbey was the home of the pioneering photographer William Henry Fox Talbot, and Lacock's medieval barn is now fittingly a museum of photographic history. Sir William Sharington died in 1553. His delicately carved monument stands in a fan-vaulted chapel of the church of St. Cyriac.

*N**ote the intricacy of the half-timbering of these overhanging houses and the old-style signpost to neighbouring places* (this page). *A local shop* (opposite) *sells memorabilia, including a tin commemorating King George VI, who died in 1952, and his bride, Lady Elizabeth Bowes-Lyon.*

"1767"
Chocolate Assortment
ST BRUNO
JAMES KEILLER & SONS
DUNDEE
MARMALADE
Virol
FLOR DE DINDIGUL
A want long felt by Smokers is a Cigar of MEDIUM
STRENGTH, POSSESSING FLAVOUR and a DELICATE AROMA
WITHOUT LEAVING AN UNPLEASANT TASTE
ST BRUNO
SLOAN'S
LINIMENT
LONDON, W.4.
MADE IN ENGLAND
SYRUP OF FIGS
CARTERS
Finest
COLD
DRAWN
CASTOR
OIL
CARTERS
ZINC
CASTOR OIL
Ointment B.P.
DIRECTIONS
APPLY FREELY TO AFFECTED PARTS
CARTERS
Antique Finished
Zinc-Alloy Miniature
DRAWING ROOM
TRADE MARK
PETAL DUST
Barling
ROYAL HUNT
25 g
TOBACCO

In the superbly vaulted Lady Chapel of the church of St. Cyriac (above) *is the resplendent Renaissance tomb of Sir William Sharington. The former abbey* (right) *was 'Gothicized' in the eighteenth century.*

Lower and Upper Slaughter

GLOUCESTERSHIRE

THE RIVER EYE divides the exquisite Cotswold villages of Lower Slaughter and Upper Slaughter, both built of honey-coloured stone, many of the buildings dating from the sixteenth and seventeenth centuries. In Lower Slaughter, St. Mary's church, a medieval foundation rebuilt in the late eighteen-sixties by Charles Shapland Whitmore, contains brass memorials to local worthies. As at Upper Slaughter, there is also very fine stained-glass.

Stroll from here beside the river to The Square, whose cottages centre on a water trough with a spout shaped like the head of a lion. Continue as far as the former nineteenth-century corn-mill (one of the few brick buildings in Lower Slaughter). Its water-wheel is still intact. From here Malthouse Lane, a street flanked by delicious cottages, runs back to The Square. Stay in the *Manor Hotel*, built in the seventeenth century, which stands opposite Manor Farm, whose present form dates from 1688.

Long ago Upper Slaughter was protected by a Norman castle, part of which still survives. In 1906 one of the finest English architects of the early twentieth century, Sir Edwin Lutyens, brilliantly remodelled a terrace of eight cottages in Baghot's Square. The parish church of St. Peter is Norman, with parts of the nave rebuilt in the fifteenth century and a chancel dating from the fourteenth. The lovely, battlemented tower is Perpendicular in style. One oddity is a fourteenth-century Easter sepulchre now housing a seventeenth-century tomb. Here are a stone screen, more fascinating tombs and nineteenth-century stained-glass.

The word 'Slaughter' has no sinister implications, but is derived from the Anglo-Saxon 'slough', which means a muddy spot, though Gallows Piece once enclosed the local scaffold.

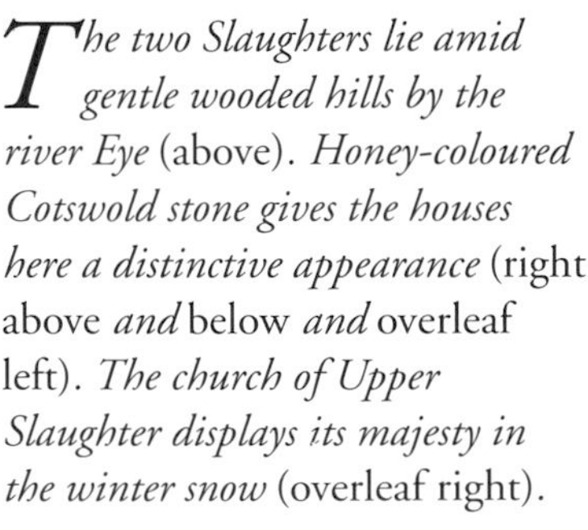

The two Slaughters lie amid gentle wooded hills by the river Eye (above). *Honey-coloured Cotswold stone gives the houses here a distinctive appearance* (right above *and* below *and* overleaf left). *The church of Upper Slaughter displays its majesty in the winter snow* (overleaf right).

This footbridge is one of two which cross the river Eye at The Slaughters (left)*; there is also a ford. The parish church of Lower Slaughter is graced with an elegant spire* (above).

Mevagissey
CORNWALL

Mevagissey and its superb harbour are sheltered by nature as well as by the results of the building skills of generations of fisherfolk (above *and* opposite).

CHARMING, though almost empty of specific architectural interest, apart from its parish church and a couple of eighteenth-century houses (Lawn House in Church Street and No.27 Polkirt Hill), Mevagissey's attraction lies in its completeness as an unspoilt Cornish fishing village. The harbour has a pier dating from the very beginning of the eighteenth century, with outer harbours added later. There are some sturdy houses, once inhabited by fisherfolk. Some of them cling to a hill. Once there was a castle here, long since destroyed. Modern houses include three in an amiably rustic style, designed by J. A. Campbell in the nineteen-thirties.

All this may seem a meagre reason for visiting the village. And yet Mevagissey should not be missed. One bonus is that its streets are so narrow and steep that most vehicles have to be left outside the village. Another is simply bathing, particularly at Polstreth to the north and at Portmellon to the south. A third is the treat of taking a trip by boat around the bay, perhaps combining this with fishing.

What of the parish church? Dedicated to two Cornish saints, St. Meva and St. Ida, it has a magnificent moulded, circular Norman font. There are fine monuments to Otwell Hill (born, as the inscription informs, in Lancashire) and his wife, dating from 1617, and to Lewis Dart, who died in 1632 and is attended by carvings of ten kneeling effigies. Hill's monument describes him as 'Franck, Frugall, Plaisant, Sober, Stout and Kinde.'

HARBOUR OFFICE
SUNSET
FY 765
FAIR IOLANTHE
FY 30
FY 30
FY431
FY424
FY 424
FY105
AQUILA FY 324
FH 16
FH 16

The harbour at Mevagissey (opposite) *is undoubtedly one of the prettiest in Cornwall. Such fishing villages first began to take shape in the fifteenth century (the first written mention of Mevagissey occurs in 1410), growing from a few scattered cottages to the tightly-knit communities of today* (this page)*, as the construction of harbours and piers followed the expansion of the fishing industry.*

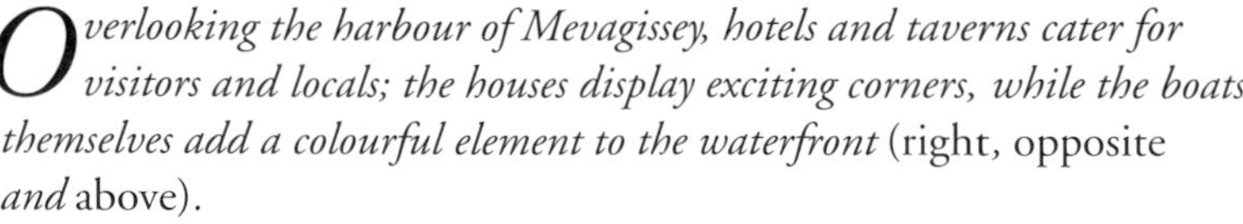

Overlooking the harbour of Mevagissey, hotels and taverns cater for visitors and locals; the houses display exciting corners, while the boats themselves add a colourful element to the waterfront (right, opposite *and* above).

Harbour Tavern
Harbour Tavern
FREE HOUSE
PUB FOOD SERVED FROM THE BAR
USHERS

HARBOUR LIGHTS
FY431
FY431
FY 30
FY779

CORNISH GOODIES
CORNISH GOODIES
WHEEL HOUSE
Coffee Gable

The harbour wall of Mevagissey, a westerly outpost of Britain's seafaring tradition, guards against the greater seas beyond. Just visible on the promontory beyond the harbour are three nineteen-thirties houses designed by J.A. Campbell (p.204). The village itself curves around the harbour, creating a picturesque cradle for the tiny fleet (pp.205–207).

SELECT BIBLIOGRAPHY

Bailey, Brian, *Stone Villages of England*, London, 1982.

Bentley, James and Rodwell, Warwick, *Our Christian Heritage*, London, 1984.

Betjeman, John ed., *Sir John Betjeman's Guide to English Parish Churches*, London, 1993.

Bourne, George, *Change in the Village*, London, 1912.

Cook, Olive, *English Cottages and Farmhouses*, London, 1982.

Eagle, Dorothy and Carnell, Hilary ed., *The Oxford Illustrated Literary Guide to Great Britain and Ireland*, Oxford, 1981.

Hadfield, John ed., *The Shell Book of English Villages*, London, 1980.

Hoskins, W.G., *The Making of the English Landscape*, London, 1955.

Muir, Richard, *The Villages of England*, London, 1992.

Ousby, Ian, *Blue Guide: England*, London, 1995.

Pevsner, Nikolaus, *The Leaves of Southwell*, London and New York, 1945.

Pevsner, Nikolaus et al., *The Buildings of England* (45 vols.), Harmondsworth, 1951–.

Roberts, Brian K., *The Making of the English Village*, Harlow, 1987.

Rowley, Trevor, *Villages in the Landscape*, London, 1978.

Seebohm, F., *The English Village Community*, London, 1883.

Taylor, Christopher, *Village and Farmstead*, London, 1983.